Odes & Offerings

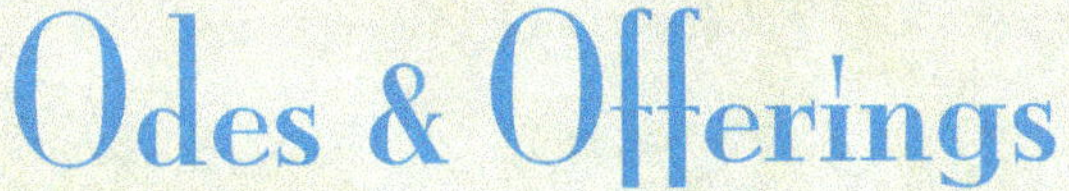

Odes & Offerings

A Collaborative Exhibit of Poetry and the Visual Arts

The City of Santa Fe's 2010-2012 Poet Laureate, Joan Logghe
and
The City of Santa Fe Arts Commission Community Gallery

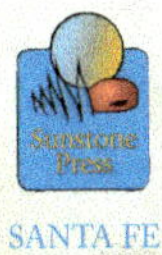

SANTA FE

Special Thanks for Generous Support of this publication to

Carl and Carol Slesinger
Sandra Deitch
Santa Fe Literary Education Fund of the Santa Fe Community Foundation

Photographs by Alex Traub

Sunstone books may be purchased for educational, business, or sales promotional use. For information please write: Special Markets Department, Sunstone Press, P.O. Box 2321, Santa Fe, New Mexico 87504-2321.

Book and Cover design › Vicki Ahl
Body typeface › Adobe Caslon Pro
Printed on acid-free paper
♾

Library of Congress Cataloging-in-Publication Data

Odes & Offerings : a collaborative exhibit of poetry and the visual arts / the City of Santa Fe's 2010-2012 Poet Laureate, Joan Logghe and the City of Santa Fe Arts Commission Community Gallery.
pages cm
ISBN 978-0-86534-955-1 (softcover-color : alk. paper)
1. American poetry--New Mexico. 2. Art and literature. I. Logghe, Joan, 1947-
PS571.N6O34 2013
811'.60809789--dc23
2013028144

WWW.SUNSTONEPRESS.COM
SUNSTONE PRESS / POST OFFICE BOX 2321 / SANTA FE, NM 87504-2321 /USA
(505) 988-4418 / ORDERS ONLY (800) 243-5644 / FAX (505) 988-1025

Contents

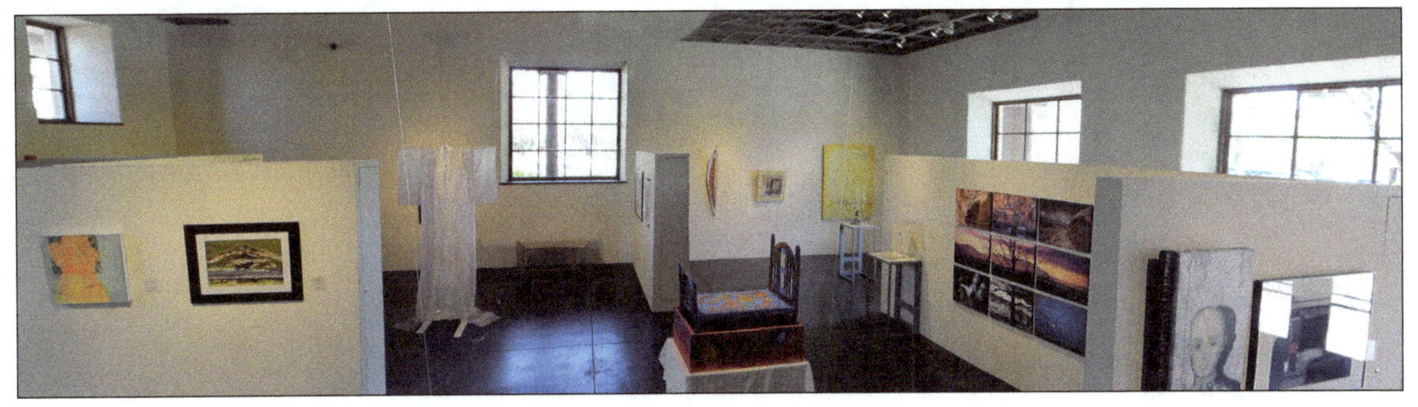

"Odes & Offerings" Gallery Installation

Foreword

"Odes & Offerings" was a unique collaboration between The City of Santa Fe Arts Commission Community Gallery, the City of Santa Fe Poet Laureate, Joan Logghe, and a host of talented local poets and artists. Conceived by Logghe in close consultation with Community Gallery Manager, Rod Lambert, the original exhibit in 2012 paired the work of a local poet with a visual artist. The results were more than just poetry-inspired artworks. Every piece became a true integration of poetry and form. With this rich, authentic cross-pollination at its core, "Odes & Offerings" became an event that brought the community of Santa Fe together around the spoken word and visual arts. This book serves as a lasting record of an inspired exhibit and the many outstanding individuals who made it possible.

Preface

I started in poetry, sitting on the stage floor of the John Hyson Presbyterian Mission School in Chimayo, where Julia Hudson, head teacher and secret wild-woman gave me a start. She allowed the combo of neo-hippie and native *Chimayoso* parents to build a solar greenhouse, bake cookies, teach weaving, celebrate Thursdays as "Beans Day" and write poetry with her students. I owe it all to her, a sweet life lived in poetry. This has nothing to do with "Odes & Offerings," except that it has everything to do with community, allowing the creative to have its ways with us, and trusting the creative life in another.

My two years as Santa Fe's third Poet Laureate were a continuation of coaxing the poems out of children, writing my own poems, or finding out how much poetry one can smuggle into non-academic lives. I had the longing for a life in poetry. Now, thirty years later poetry has delivered me the feast of two years at the poetry smorgasbord and this is a full banquet, not a continental breakfast. Poetry has taken me to Keynote at Santa Fe High Graduation, my matriarchal appearance, with grandkids, at the Fourth of July Pancake Breakfast, Labor Day poems, a City Council poem, two years of nursing home appearances for Valentine's Day with three hundred handmade cards and a passel of friends, and many schools reaching hundreds of elementary students with musician Jeremy Bleich in "Joan and the Giant Pencil." We made a program that models enthusiasm for what one loved as a child, in my case poetry, lasting into adulthood. A poetry performance was a project I had been thinking about for years and with this poetry feast it moved to the front burner. An honorary position such as Poet Laureate is a chance to bring to the front burner those projects we think we don't have the time or resources to accomplish. People love the role. It's a Jungian city and this is an archetype. I feel honored to have stood inside its projection and power.

"Odes & Offerings" was a fleeting thought that turned into a full experience of several art forms. I knew visual artists who were bringing text into their work: Piper Leigh's kimonos, Sabra Moore's structures and books, Suzanne Vilmain's books and environments, Axle

Contemporary's Haiku Roadsign, and Julie Wagner's art, rich in text. What if they were asked to incorporate the words of poets from the Santa Fe community? With the backing of the City of Santa Fe Arts Commission and its Community Gallery I got the go ahead on this show.

I invited thirty-six poets, a number Community Gallery Manager, Rod Lambert, and I arrived at as optimal. The selection was a challenge as I have so many lasting friendships and poetry students, but was not able to invite everybody whose work I loved and respected. Every week I would be in a state about another poet who came to mind. I thank those who participated and those who I was unable to include: the creative will find a way. I know they will make projects of their own. Each poet sent four poems and I selected two of them.

Rod sent out the call for the artists and had a great response. Thirty-six artists were chosen from a pool of ninety. The most collaborative moments were in meeting with Rod and a stack of work by thirty-six poets and the portfolios of thirty-six artists. There were ones that had to be: Sabra Moore with Santana Shorty, both Abiquiu women. Sabra, an amazing sculptor and artist book maker from the New York Women's art collective Heresy of the 1970s, and Santana, known as a stunning performing artist with the Santa Fe Indian School Spoken Word Team. Indeed the piece embodies all I had envisioned for this show.

I could tell you, one by one, how we made the matches—by sensibilities, thematic matters, friendships or at random. The next morning I realized that in the case of two of my closest friends, my vision had been clouded and I messed up, the technical term. If I could just switch the two artists, it would be the last jigsaw piece in place. And so we did. The artists had to wrestle now, with the poems. Each piece was made specifically for the exhibit.

Besides our gallery show, a smaller show opened on Canyon Road at GVG Contemporary owned by one of the artists, Blair Vaughn-Gruler. She called it "Odes & Offerings, Deconstructed." It gave a glimpse into the process of ten of the artists and their poets.

Odes are poems of praise. Keats, Milton, and Pablo Neruda come to mind. An offering is a more complex human impulse. It is the gift into the community, in this case made by its poets and artists, over and over, day after precious day, that makes Santa Fe the City of Holy

Faith. It's not only the light, it is the generosity. The poets offered up their words for transformation, letting the poems go as they may. The artists gave of their resources, very deeply.

The opening drew six hundred people, give or take a few hundred. I tend to underestimate. You couldn't budge. I stood at the mobbed entrance handing out name tags. I didn't even venture out except to have a photo taken with my artist, Bernadette Freeman. I lost my voice. But guess what? Julia Hudson, that beloved two room schoolhouse teacher, and one of the "Ten Who Made A Difference in Santa Fe," was there. She definitely made a difference in my life. Her presence made the fabric whole.

My thanks go to the Poet Laureate program of the City of Santa Fe Arts Commission, to Sabrina Pratt, Rod Lambert, and the staff. To former Arts Commissioner, Marilyn Batts, who was an instigator for the program. To Steven Schwartz and the Witter Bynner Foundation for Poetry for supporting the Poet Laureate program both spiritually and financially. To the LEF and Vessel Foundations for support, so I could say many more yeses to invitations to read and travel. Tom Leech and James Bourland of the Palace Press for broadsides, books, and hosting events at the New Mexico Museum of History. To Carl and Carol Slesinger, Sandra Deitch and the Santa Fe Literary Education Fund of the Santa Fe Community Foundation for support of this book. To Sunstone Press for all the poets it has given ink, and seeing this show immediately as page worthy The city loves having a Laureate. It's not personal, it's poetic.

—Joan Logghe, Santa Fe Poet Laureate, 2010–2012

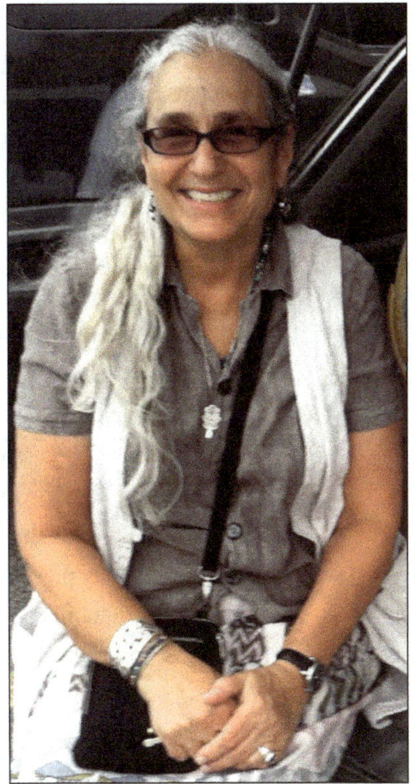

Santa Fe's Poet Laureate 2010–2012, Joan Logghe, photograph by Piper Leigh

Introductions

The impact and innovation of "Odes & Offerings" as an exhibit concept for The City of Santa Fe Arts Commission Community Gallery was unprecedented. Attendance on opening night, March 23, 2012, was an example of controlled mayhem and visitors to the Community Gallery were both inspired and opinionated, but above all, engaged.

I have to admit that I experienced initial skepticism in the early development stages of the project that the exhibit wouldn't resonate with the community. Call me a downer, a worrier or a pessimist, but my job description includes "concern" as a required skill set.

My primary concerns were two-fold:

How will local artists respond to the specified request of incorporating the content of poems into the landscape of their current bodies of work? (Would anyone even be interested?)

Will the nature of a singularly text-driven exhibit result in an exhibit of predominantly two-dimensional works, creating a less textural experience for the viewer?

Despite these concerns, we pressed on with Joan Logghe's selection for participating poets and a public call for artists' portfolios. We rolled the dice and placed our bets, hoping for big returns. Joan's selection process for poets was not an enviable one in any number of ways and the selection of artists was no easier.

A function of the Community Gallery's exhibit programming is that artists are asked to create a single art piece responding to a selected theme. Historically, I find that artists sometimes feel constrained by their collector base, market expectations or simply, their own fears, and often find themselves producing a body of work that becomes repetitive and "safe." In contrast, artists who participate in Community Gallery exhibits are forced to explore a new theme or a new medium, get out of their comfort zone, gain a different perspective and speak with a fresh voice. I jokingly refer to it as "dancing in a new pasture." The Community Gallery removes the typical constraints artists face in their everyday careers and replaces them with foreign thematic "fences" that force them to work in a new and exciting way. Whether the process simply tweaks an artistic process or refocuses an artist's creative methods, the result is inspired play that is endlessly fascinating to watch. This exhibit was no different.

In fact, "Odes & Offerings" pushed the participating artists into tighter creative quarters than ever before, resulting in a body of work that was engaging, exciting and inspired. If one considers the constraints of translating poetic phrases and stanzas into a work of art without too literally or directly interpreting them and having to simultaneously pay respect to the poet and their work, this collaborative process was, at best, in a word, daunting. Fortunately, the Community Gallery's Advisory Committee, who are responsible for the selection of exhibit themes and the participating artists, always surprise but never disappoint me with their selections. Of the overwhelming number of submitted artists' portfolios (ninety) they innately understood who was up for the challenge. My first concern was unwarranted. The results spoke for themselves.

"Odes & Offerings," as an exhibit, challenged me as well. From an installation perspective, there were eleven sculptures, nine mixed media pieces, a video as well as a healthy smattering of digital, fiber, drawing and traditional paintings. The dizzying range and variety of media submitted for the exhibit instantly eliminated my second concern. Instead of becoming a two-dimensional and possibly flat, exhibit, the incorporation of the written word didn't confine the texture of this exhibit at all. In stark contrast, the results delivered by this talented and varied group of artists were a feast of sight, sound and tactile experiences that, as a curator, were a sheer joy to install. It was exciting to bring these seemingly disparate components together in a cohesive way, creating a chorus of voices (both poet and artist) while simultaneously allowing each individual piece the opportunity for a solo.

Joan was a creative, visionary force to partner with on this exhibit which ran from March 23, 2012 to June 8, 2012. From the early development phases of the project throughout the run of "Odes & Offerings" programming, we were able to dream big, work hard and play well together in an effort to pay tribute to both poets and artists working in New Mexico. The response from the community was overwhelming and the confirmation of Joan's vision and our efforts were recognized, praised and thankfully received by our visitors.

I guess I worry too much.

—Rod Lambert
The City of Santa Fe Arts Commission, Community Gallery Manager

Santa Fe is fortunate to have a wealth of writers and authors. According to the National Endowment for the Arts publication titled *Artists in the Workforce 1990–2005*, Santa Fe is first among the top ten metropolitan areas ranked by percentage of writers and authors in the workforce. We don't have a count of poets, but we know that there are many—and even more important, there is a large audience interested in poetry.

Our Poet Laureate program has had surprising and amazing results. In 2004 The City of Santa Fe Arts Commission was doing strategic planning, and Commission Chair Marilyn Batts brought up the idea of having a Poet Laureate position within the City of Santa Fe. She thought that it would serve to raise the profile of the literary arts in our community. We had no idea how effective a poet laureate program can be.

We set the work of Santa Fe's Poet Laureate to include readings at official City functions and community events, as well as a community outreach project. The readings might be of a new poem at the swearing-in ceremony for the Mayor and City Councilors, or poetic observations about Santa Fe at the annual July 4th Pancake Breakfast on Santa Fe's downtown plaza, or a work selected for the ribbon cutting at a new community park. The community outreach projects have been poetry readings, workshops and exhibits.

Joan Logghe served as Santa Fe's third Poet Laureate from 2010–2012. Building on the excellent work done by Arthur Sze (2006–2008) and Valerie Martínez (2008–2010), Logghe did an outstanding job of raising awareness of poetry and educating young children. An inspiring passion for poetry allows her to connect with people of all ages and backgrounds. Her performance "Joan and the Giant Pencil" was extremely popular with elementary school audiences. She received numerous invitations to participate in community happenings. Her reading of "April in Santa Fe" at a City Council meeting was received enthusiastically. Pairing artists with the work of poets turned out to be an over the top idea that had a great impact on all involved.

"Odes & Offerings" was one of the most well-received exhibits The City of Santa Fe Arts Commission Community Gallery has hosted. There was a record crowd for the opening reception and a steady stream of visitors in the weeks following. The artists juried into this exhibit took the unusual challenge of using a phrase or an entire poem in their visual art and ran with it. The works of art, as you'll see in this book, are full of meaning provided by the poems. Joan's thoughtful approach to matching poets with artists resulted in an unusually popular exhibit of work. We are fortunate to live in an area where we have many exemplary artists and writers.

The Arts Commission's goal of raising the profile of the literary arts has been met by Joan Logghe's generous approach to working in the community and being involved with audiences of all ages. "Odes & Offerings" is the culmination of two years of intense activity warmly received by the public. Please enjoy this book of poetry and art.

—Sabrina V. Pratt
Former Director, The City of Santa Fe Arts Commission

Odes & Images

Jack's Creek Soliloquy

Tommy Archuleta

Aspen leaves
blowing over a closed mining road,

someone's sec ret fishing hole down below
practicing its one-note solo—

if a man can't reconfirm his actions
here, then where can he?

She hadn't the will to pull
the Colt's hammer back, so I did.

The report itself, a tap really
with a flame tied to it.

———

You never get used to the sound
of a toy piano going
long after the shot turns blue

A curse for some, I suppose, a prayer for those of us
given to God's darker arias;

how they bless bum canals
while fiddling with our poor machinery
the chief mystery.

———

I hope a warm spray of ivory light
overtook her visual field,

that as she approached
a portal appeared
revealing the treeline of a new forest.

One with pine crowns not as marred as these
from the banquets of archangels.

Hope her ghost when it arrives
brings food, for I brought none worth sharing.

———

You know
they found a man not far from here
his boots were off
a note pinned to his chest
the paper said he drank and drank
himself to death
no word as to how much self-loathing
was in his blood stream
I couldn't be anymore tired
How about you

———

Whatever comes next
one of us had better build a fire,

the other tend to it
on through the coming, irreversible frost.

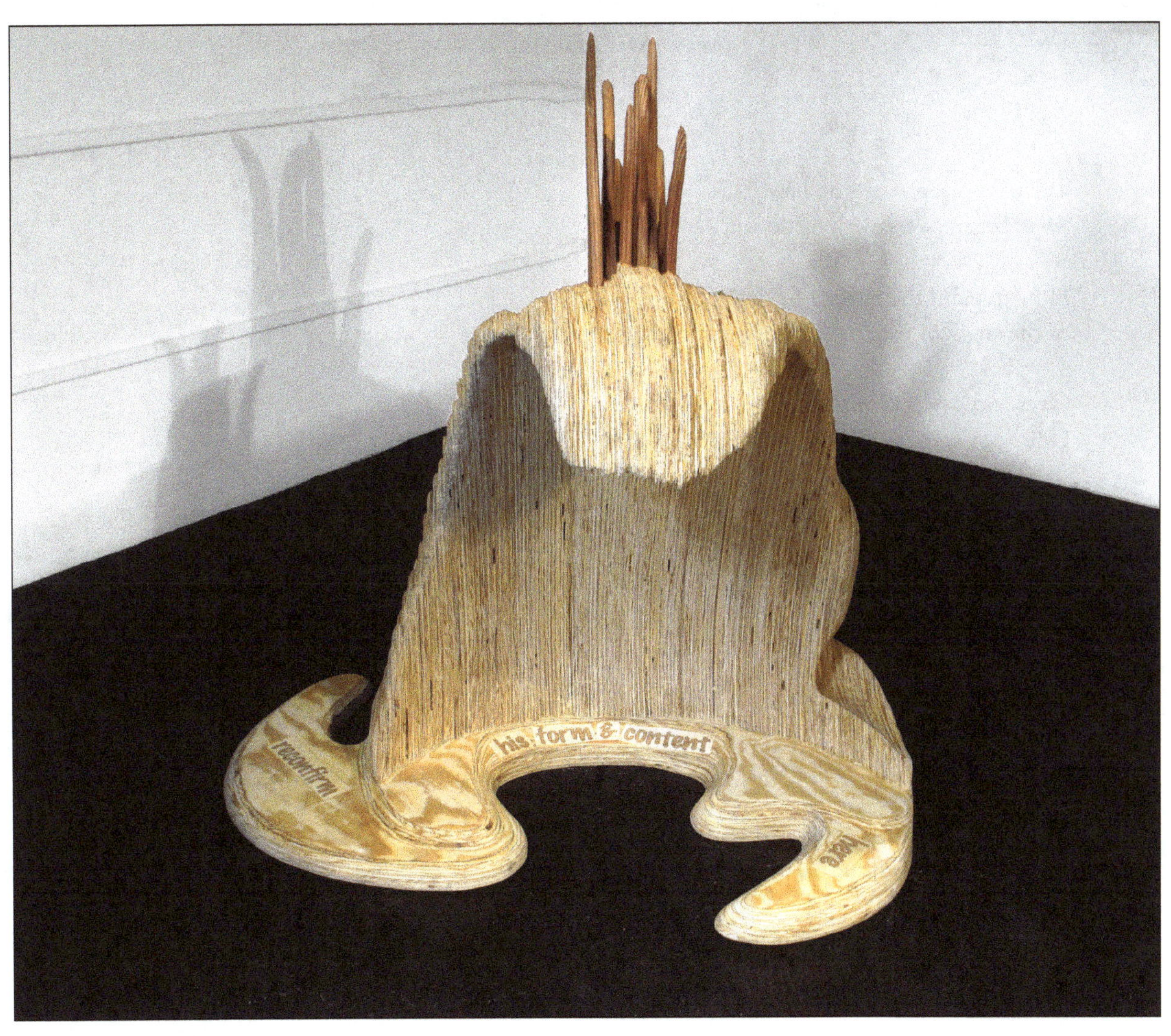

Dana Chodzko, "Reconfirm," mixed laminated wood, 5 x 5 x 5'

After Li Ch'ing-chao
John Brandi

The river disappears into haze,
a wet brush swells with oxide and pearl.

How to paint the taste of fine rain
or the small of your back through prismed silk?

Over and over, point the tip.
One after another, tear sheets from the pad.

In twilight, beyond the open door
a slippery path glistens.

Far below, the trail twists.
Hill after hill recedes into mist.

The lamp grows dim, the wind
beats steady on the shutters.

My hand shakes
as it traces your outline on the page.

The wine has spilled, the brush is too far
and I am too close to see.

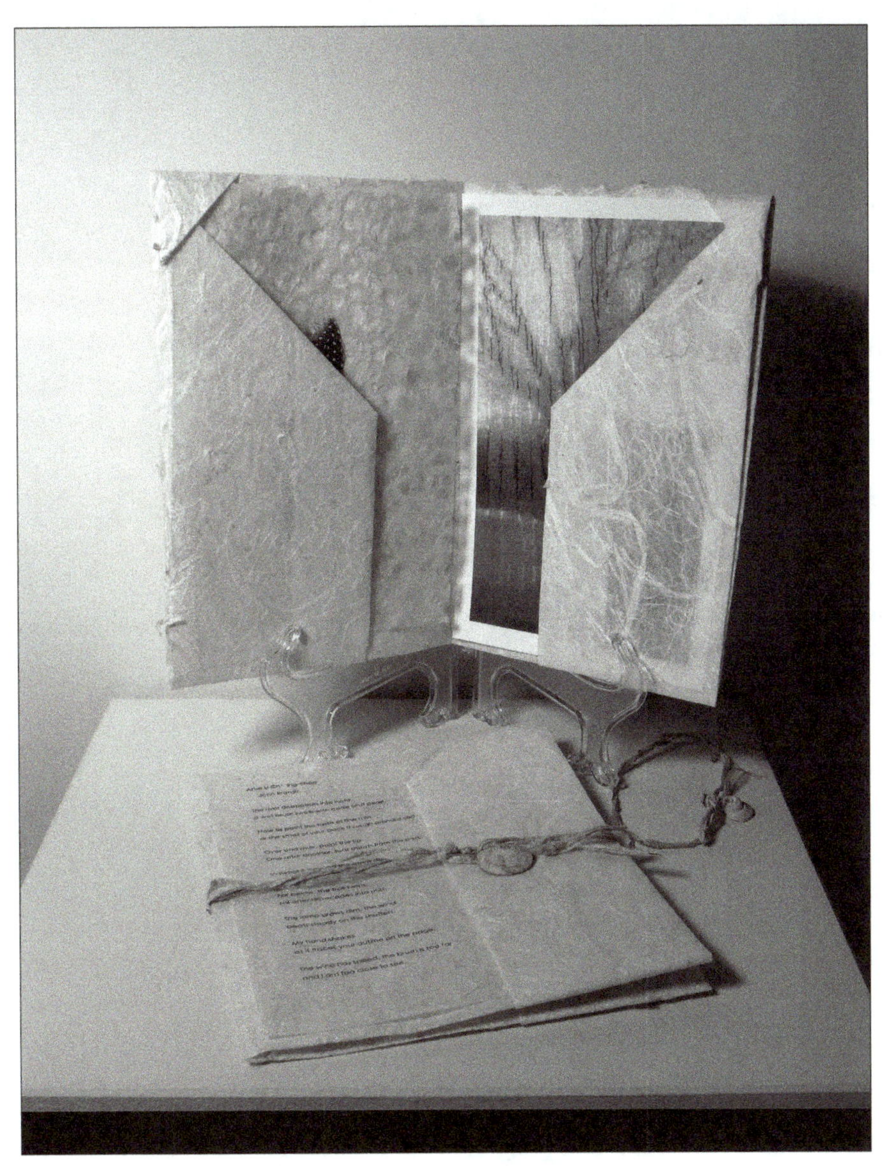

Gail Rieke, "Rain Window Portfolio," mixed media, 12 x 9 x 1"

Get Stirred
Debbi Brody

What does next smell like?
A sweet storm washed in rapture
or lightning in a field of onions?

Turn ghetto ash into esoterica, fill a vase with rocks.
Make a deep cradle of buttons and wood.

Male wind sifts like silt through a card game.
Female sand drifts through arroyos, shuffles
daisies, symphonies, wasps, nectar.

Poems get out there, to Moab, to somewhere
in Texas, then back to Albuquerque and Santa Fe.

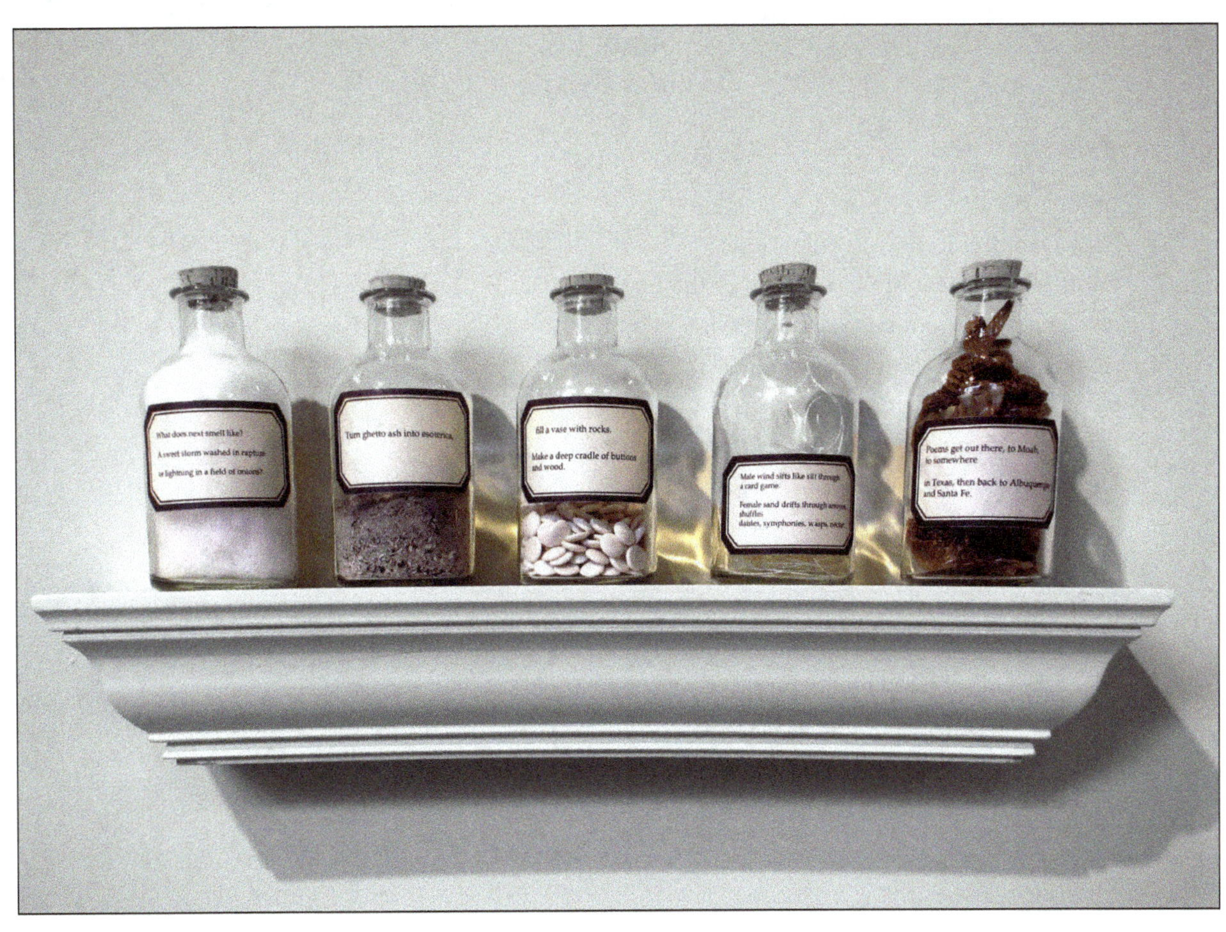

Bunny Tobias, "Get Stirred," mixed media, 24 x 11 x 5"

Santa Fe
Witter Bynner

Among the automobiles and in a region
Now Democratic, now Republican,
With a department-store, a branch of the Legion,
A Chamber of Commerce and a moving-van,
In spite of cities crowding on the Trail,
Here is a mountain-town that prays and dances
With something left, though much besides may fail,
Of the ancient faith and wisdom of St. Francis.

His annual feast has come. His image moves
Along these streets of people. And the trees
And kneeling women, just as they did before,
Welcome and worship him because he proves
That natural sinners put him at his ease,
And so he enters the cathedral-door.

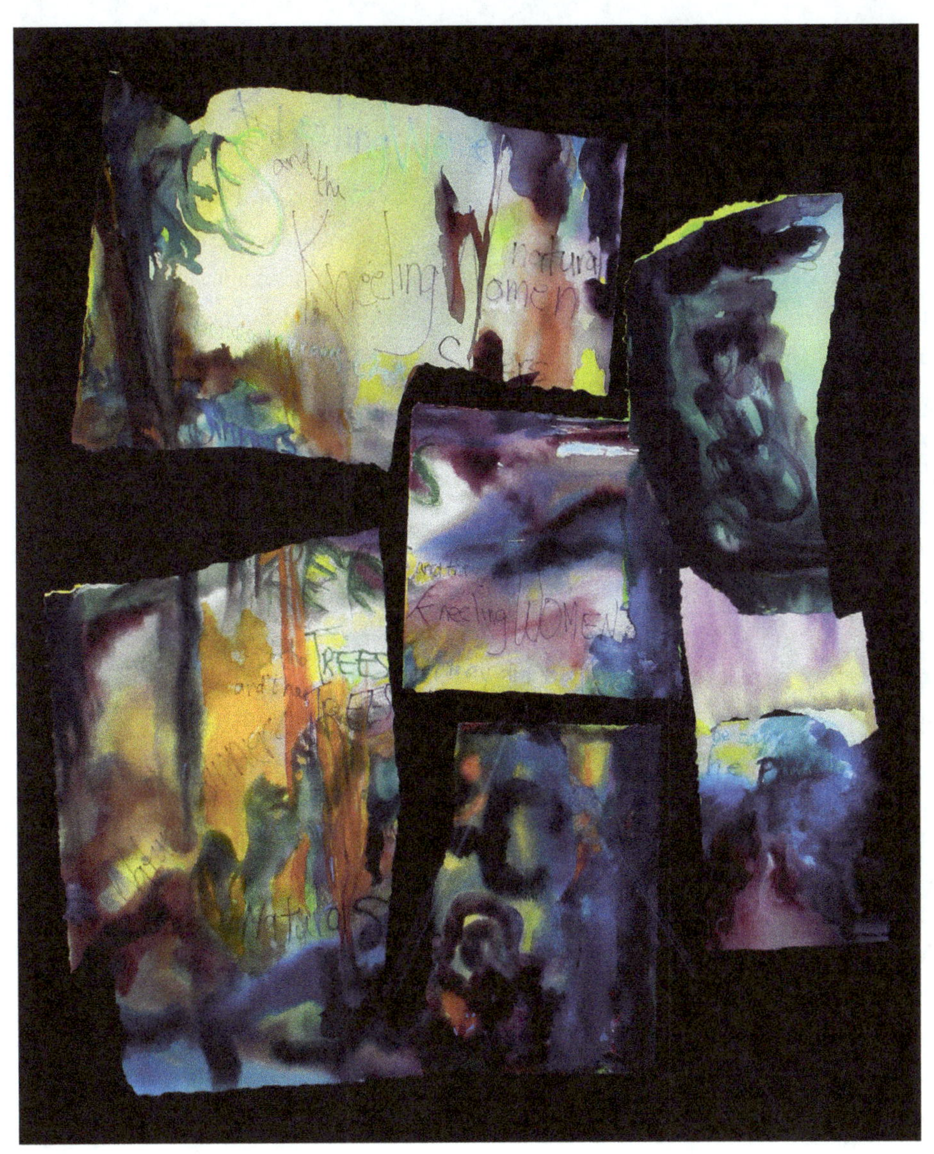

Jane Shoenfeld, “Kneeling Woman,” mixed media, 32 x 40”

Under A Yellowwood Tree

Lauren Camp

She moves slowly
through the emerald meadow
of grass in her back yard.
Hunched in memory, she is
almost seeds. I am with her
but she is alone, under
her yellowwood tree, facing west
into the rim of desert sun.
We are strangers strolling
this fertile soil. Decades ago,
she planted the book of life
and added daily to its chapters,
clearing her acre of prickles and
blemishes, turning the ground
with wonder. As trees lengthened
into sky, her little boys married
and moved away. Now, the many
pages of her story grow around her.
She surveys the flourishing garden:
golden aspens and agapanthus,
the plutonium corner of felted
horehound, bishop's weed and
yarrow. I read the landscape of lines
on her face, each furrow cultivated
into years. Finches and jays
ricochet past, shouting and squawking;
the air collages into a bright mosaic
of feathers. The woman's eyes wilt,
lids nearly translucent, her voice,
a series of tiny wingbeats
as she leafs casually through
bits and parts of herself. I lean in
to catch her words, but the wind soughs
and carries them away. Daylight
curves to dusk; she is sloping
into darkness. In a moment I will
return to my friends just
beginning to scratch the surface
of their lives. But this is satisfying,
watching this woman, as her shadow
blooms into a luminous spectrum,
though her blossoms
are long since spent.

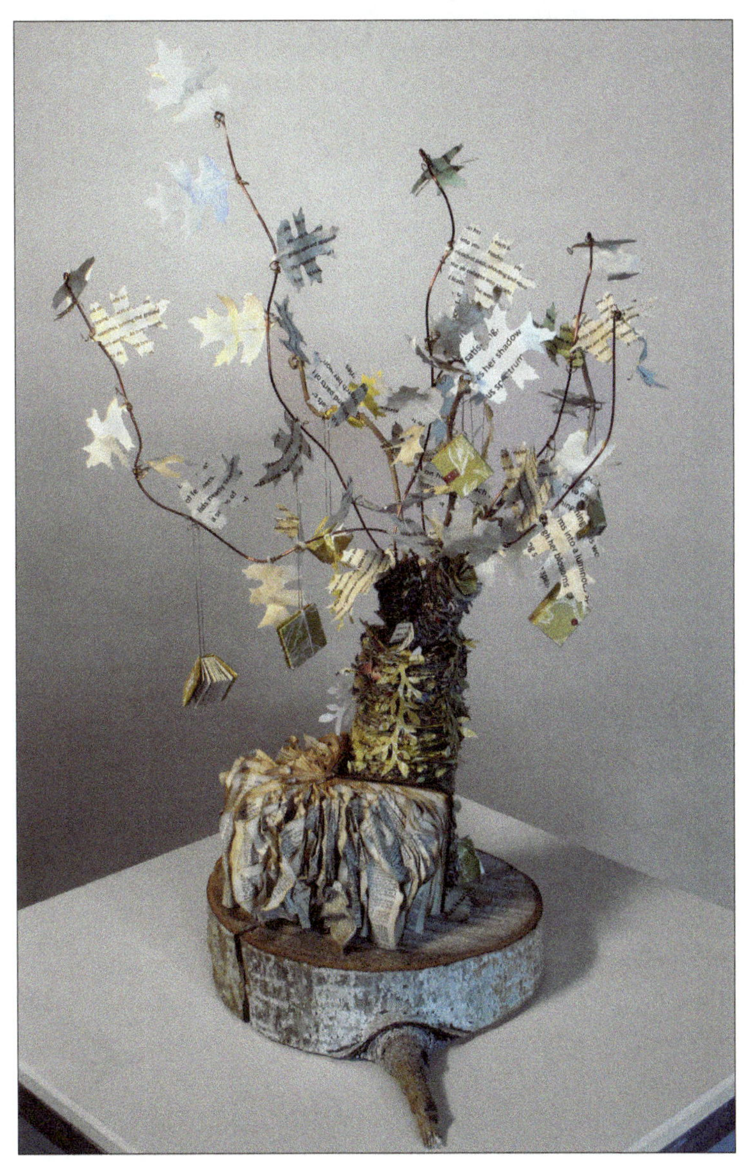

Joy Campbell, "The Yellowwood Tree," mixed media, 23 x 15 x 14"

Eva and the Birds
Sudasi J. Clement

Mid-dream you knock,
your small silhouette in the doorway.
You tell me your mother has shattered
into a thousand pieces, offer cupped hands
for me to see. Porcelain slivers transform
into fluttering birds. Swift, sparrow,
starling—we watch them fly.

Some mornings you sift
through the cool sand, gritty world
of peaks and valleys. Afternoons we climb
Piñon Ridge to study the shifting clouds:
a feather, a wing, a bird. You search
with one eye over mountains and mesas,
the other is afraid to look.

There's a juniper tree on the ridge.
When you climb her, many birds come,
so close you whisper secrets. The birds
leave abruptly, the pull of their wings
making music out of air. We walk home
at dusk, feather twirling in your fingers,
green eyes on the sky.

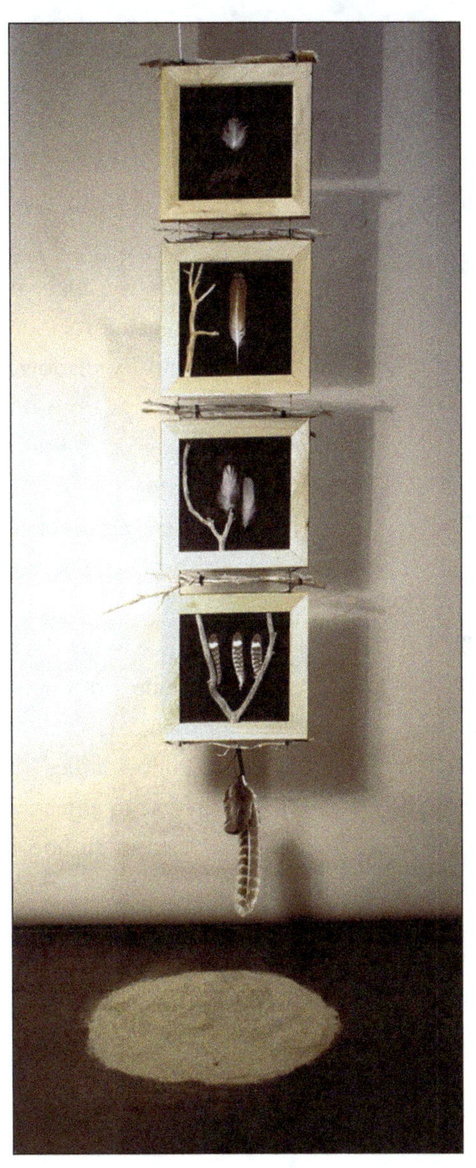

Bobbe Besold, "Birds and Eva and the Birds," mixed media, 4.5' x 1' x 1"

Janice and the Goats
Catherine Ferguson

From my bed last night I heard Janice's goats kick
  the shelves of their pens, overturn the shallows
    of water boats.
One of me got up, gathered weeds from the ledges
  of rock walls, split the coyote melon vines
    and stepped through peninsulas of dream
  to bring them food.
One of me lay in the cinders of forest fire and beat
  the earth till the goats came running.

Janice woke to my jar of lavender flowers beside her bed.
I said, I am studying the topography of goat.

One of the goats is an old historian of the mountains.
The other, black and white, wears a watermelon leash.
The old one's horns twist two icebergs meeting sideways.
Cupid dances on their ears, Janice loves, and gathers
  the reins. I want to draw.

She pastures them beside the waterfall. They poke
with their hooves sliding cascades of undissolved sand.
The old one eats Janice's shirt off her body.
I stare through Russian olive leaves, a curtain
  of gray mist obscuring the naked peaks of her breasts.

The old goat is the color of buttered toast.
From the cliff balcony a raven dips like a sailor
  into the chalky arroyo.
Janice's throat and sternum are covered with desert
  jewelry shadows.
She says, do you want to come to my house for coffee?
The goats follow our word-crumbs of spangled pastry.

Our lives divided by the deaths of our men.
Our lives answered now by goats, and dogs.

Janice wears the tattoos of leaves on her chest.
We bow through the entrances of willow swamps.
The goats swallow the river. I want to drink.
I follow Janice into the yard where the goats
refuse to enter their pen,
stamp their hooves for hot coffee.

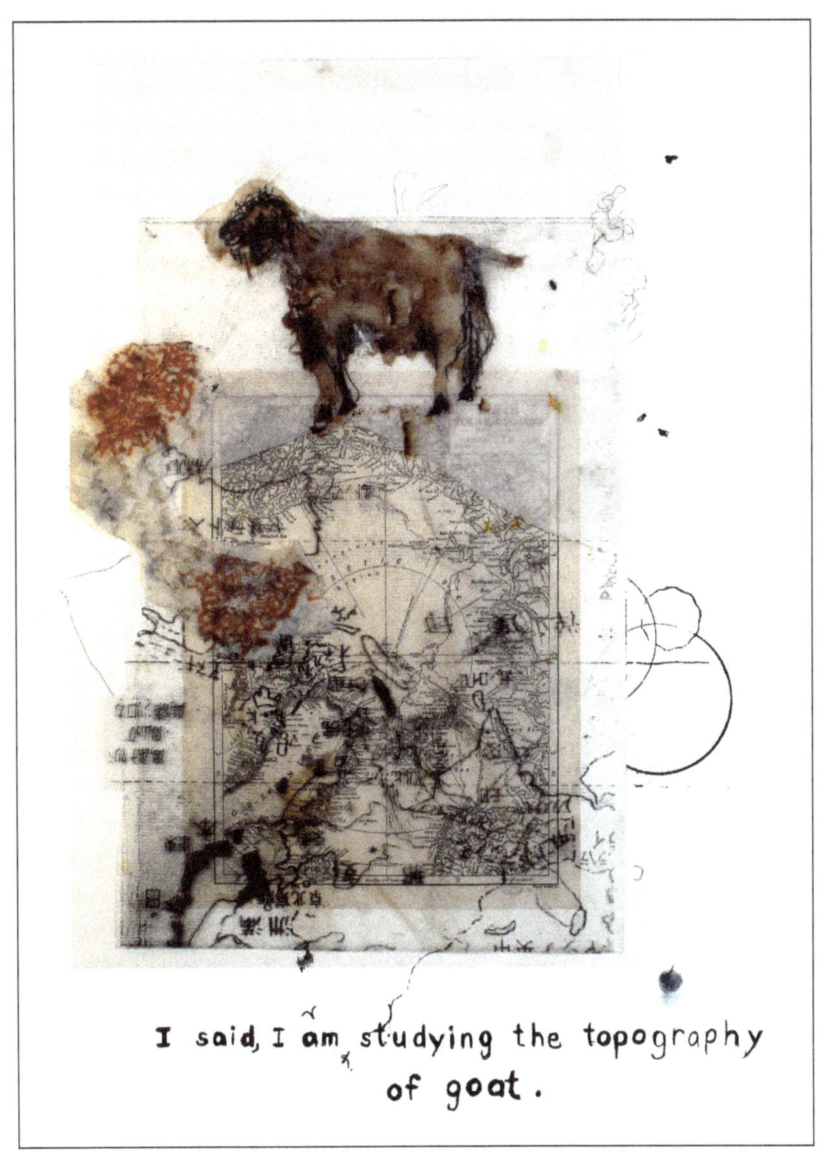

Kathleen McCloud, "Historian of the Mountains," mixed media on paper, 30 x 22"

Pons asinorum
Phil Geronimo

The corners of the room bring us to the point,
  Where we suffocate. Or—
Is it escape from this self-contained blindness.

On the bedroom desktop
  A pomegranate sits
On prose by Robbins.

No, Solzhenitsyn.

The pomologist once won acclaim for his punica granatam.

The poly-rhythms of the next room remind him of his solitude.

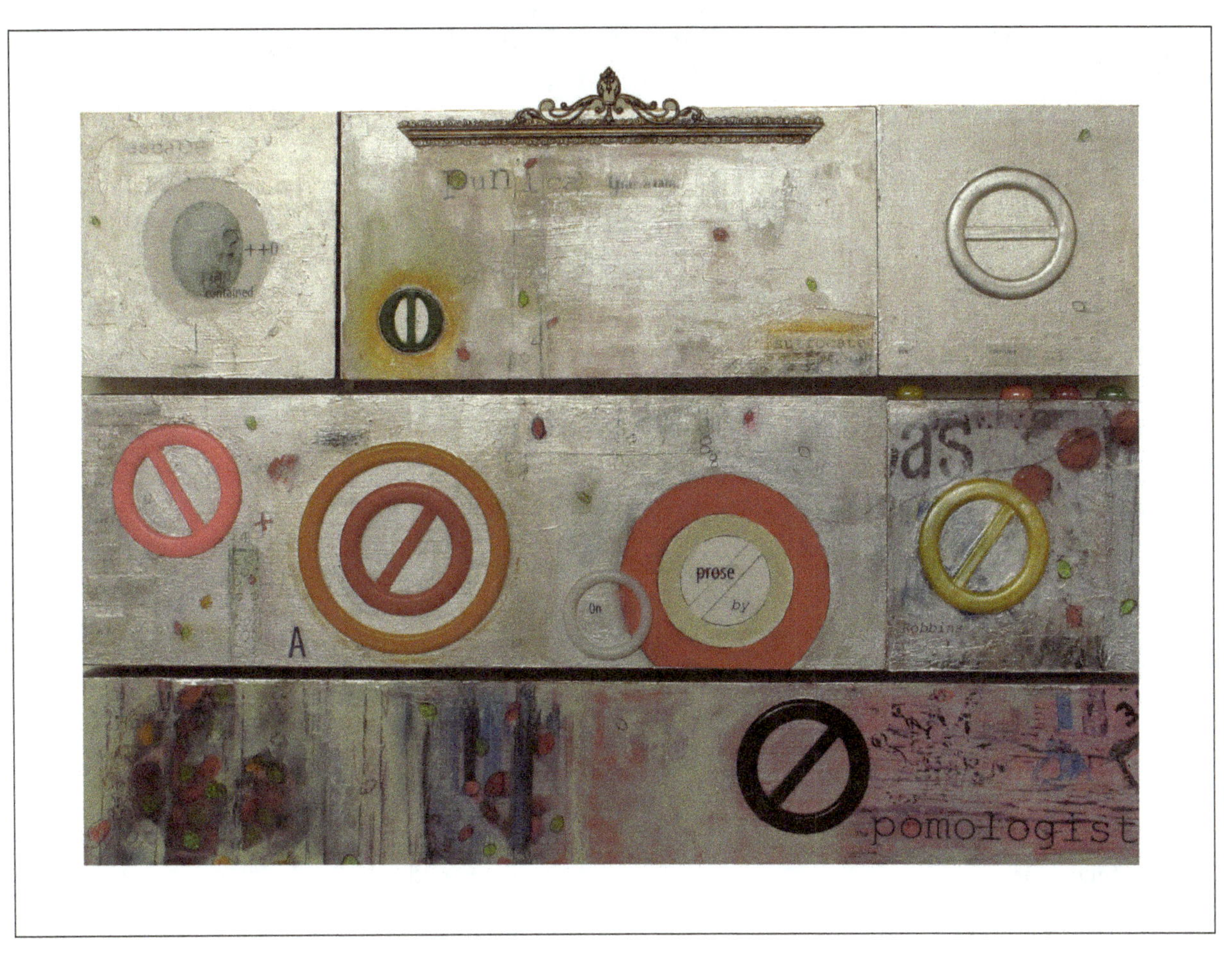

Brenda Roper, "Prose by Robbins," mixed media on panel, 18 x 24 x 2"

Ode to Turquoise
Jenice Gharib

What
gnarled
and dirt-stained
hands
searched
in the mother soil
until
they found
your blue vein.
Carried you
from Persia
China, Egypt,
and Cerrillos,
to peer
at me
from behind
store windows,
follow me
on the arms
of strangers.
Brother to coral.
Lover to silver.
You bring
the dream
of water
to an
arid land.
You lend
your beauty
to the peacock,
the palace,
and the sea.
Some robin
has lost
her egg.
Some spider
her web.
You have
dispelled
the darkness.
Tear
of the
blue-skinned god,
you are
the holy stone,
the sign
of heaven
on earth.

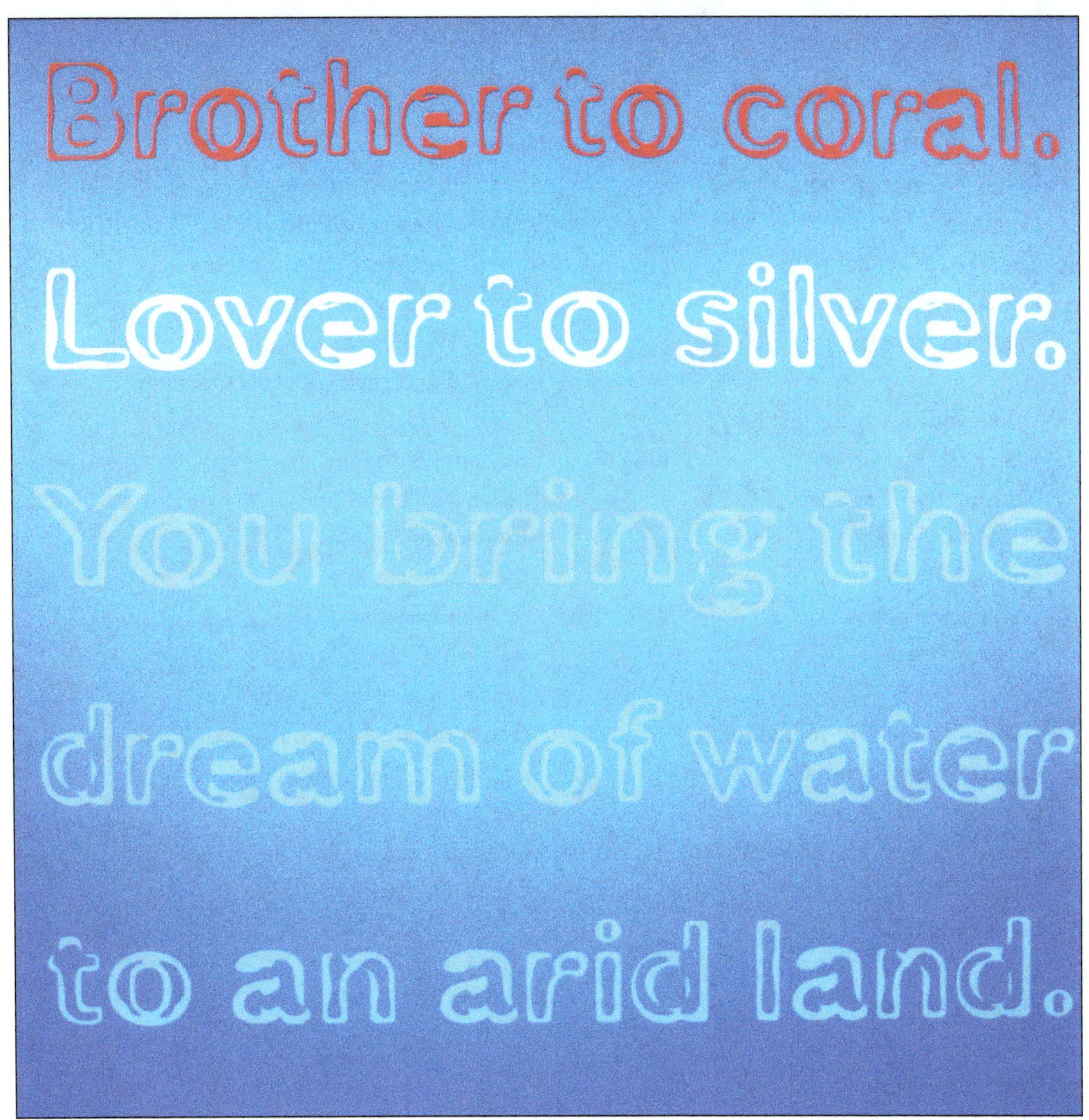

Roger Green, "Ode to Turquoise," mixed media on canvas, 36 x 36"

Dance With Me
Natalie Goldberg

When you run up against love
Watch it!
You'll never get out of it
Like bird marks on sand
it'll never leave

When you run up against love
Watch it!
Nothing'll sink as deep
or want so long
Spring so high
Never settle down
as love

It'll be like rocks in your garden
Cracks on your sidewalk
Car wheels turning
That's how fast it'll run you down!

So don't eat salt
and don't ever eat love!
Don't sit on love
or hold it like a pillow
Love will destroy
I know it

So have some tea
here sit with me
the breeze outside's fine
windows are open
We'll dance tonight
like curtains & arms touching

So dance with me
heave your breath in
Remember the toes!
those dots in a line
& ankle bones

Music on the street
rain in the air
rain hitting black pavement
like music
like light on ice cubes
Come and dance with me!

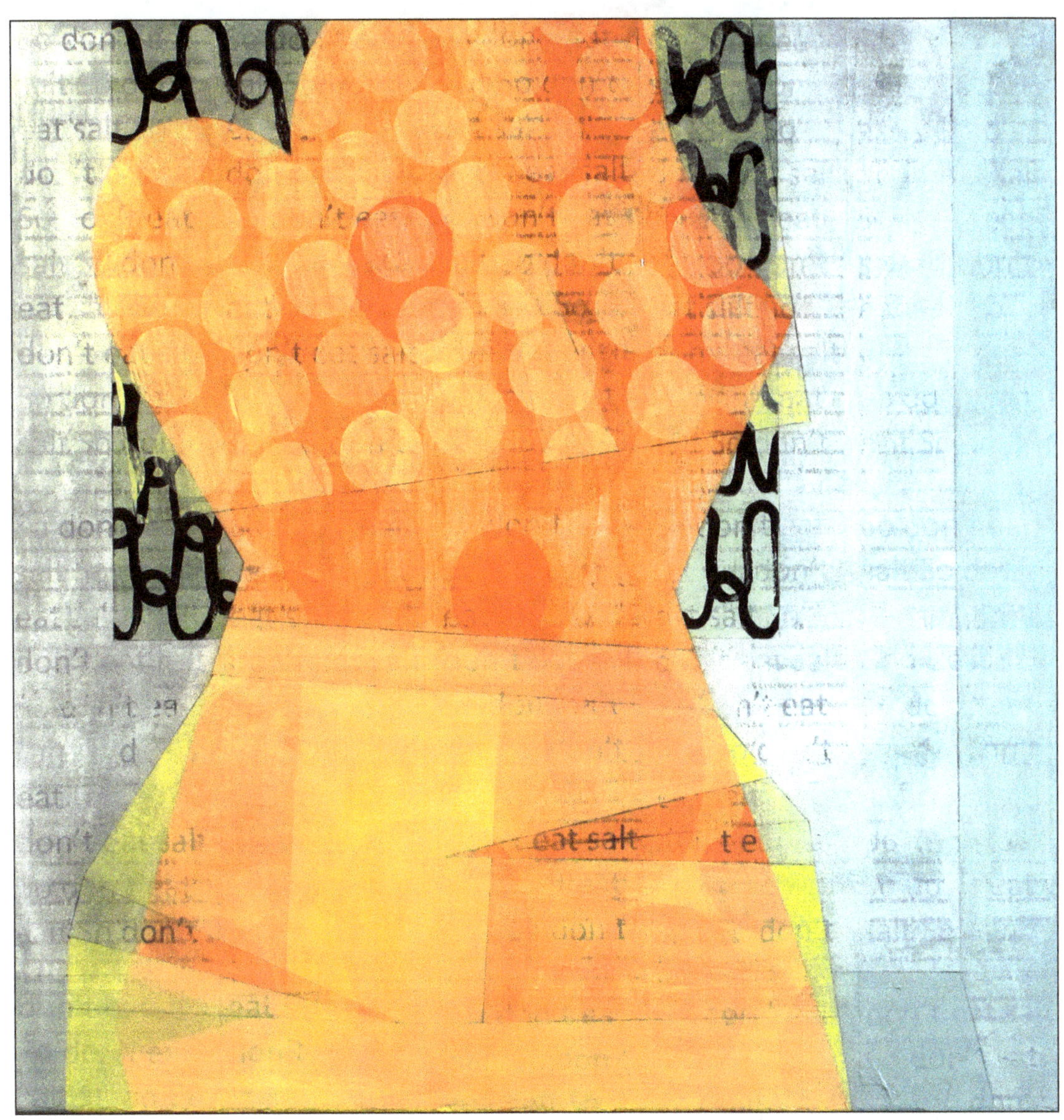

Kuzana Ogg, "Nimahk," oil on canvas, 20 x 20"

Sometimes

Renée Gregorio

Sometimes the sunset is all I can bear,
that rosy golden light all I need to know
of what the world can do to you.
The bright pink and white cosmos refuse
to look less cheerful in the shadows.
On the aging wooden table, dried out
from this desert air, cracking and changing shape,
I have two candles here in front of me:
one for the burgeoning underbelly of earth
beneath my spreading feet, the other
for quieting the world's solid confusion,
when going to war is for peace's sake.
Sometimes I think of the men I've loved
and how each was perfect and necessary,
for a time, how I'm always looking in,
then looking out, till I wake up dizzy
with the thought of what's possible and impossible,
and I want to eat homemade vanilla ice cream
with toasted coconut and caramel sauce
till I die in the sweet delight of it all.
Sometimes the changing air of fall could make me
break down, crack open. Sometimes if
I could play the piano again, and sing,
I'd hit the road with these poems,
I'd call up my fourth cousin, Chick Corea,
and have him show me the show-biz ropes,
I'd have dinner with everyone I've ever loved
gone to the other side now and there'd be
no pressure to be anything other than what I am,
conflicted and bright as the New Mexico sunflowers
that won't blossom, then do,
under the half-mooned, Milky-Way sky,
wanting nothing but the sun to rise again
        over these hills.

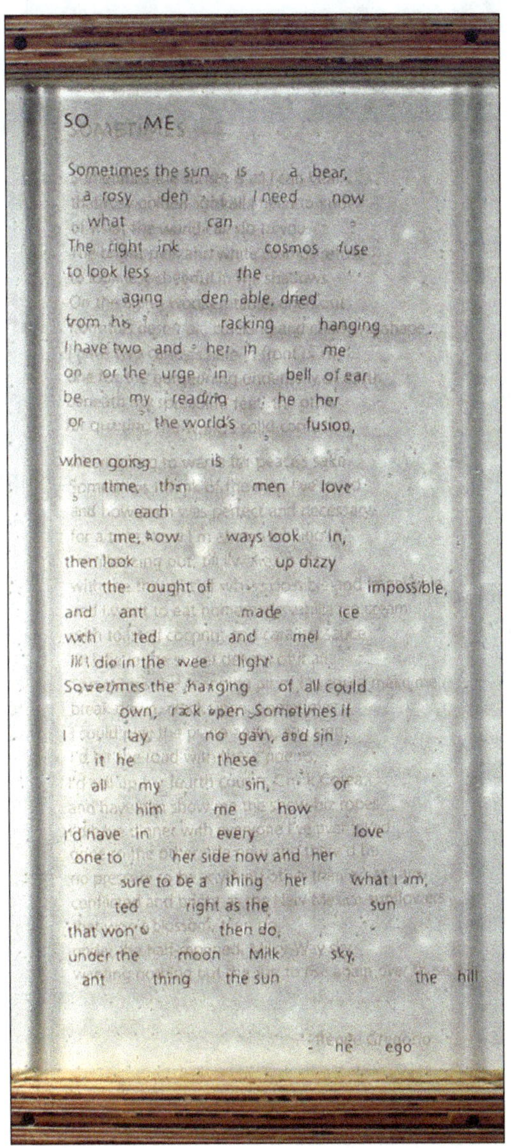

Matthew Chase-Daniel, "Sometimes So/Me," glass, 24 x 12 x 3"

The Mesa the Shadow Built
Judyth Hill

There are very few landscapes as urgent as shadow,
though some can be traced on the smooth skin of apple.
That curve so like the picked clean bone
we found that day we walked the mesa.
Our last step, with horizon as doorway,
we walked into distance as if into delirium.

We were called into that delirium
by slanting rays of steel gray shadow
that opened the sunlight into doorway
reminding us vaguely of the sheen on ripe apple,
a scent that followed us up on the mesa
creatures worrying a favored bone.

You're wondering if we found that bone,
or threw it down in our delirium.
But the Pedernal is not just any mesa,
and the light there isn't a skin to shadow.
To paint or not is the question of apples
that turns a canvas into doorway.

It doesn't take a genius to recognize doorway.
Though it took O'Keeffe to see a bone.
Cezanne painted apple after apple,
producing a mountain and his own delirium.
All the while, light required shadow,
just as horizon demands a mesa.

Georgia demanded a mesa,
and walked through light as if a doorway
which is to say, she practiced seeing the shadow
that light has wrought inside bone.
The stillness she painted is the opposite of delirium
I mean it. It's a glamour of apple.

No, don't bother with apple.
Instead, head out and climb the mesa.
That is the journey that quiets delirium,
transforming darkness into doorway –
the way we know it in our bones,
the way we see the gleam in shadow.

Remember to taste shadow in autumn's first apple.
Drum moonlight with bone long abandoned to mesa,
that music, a doorway leading back from delirium.

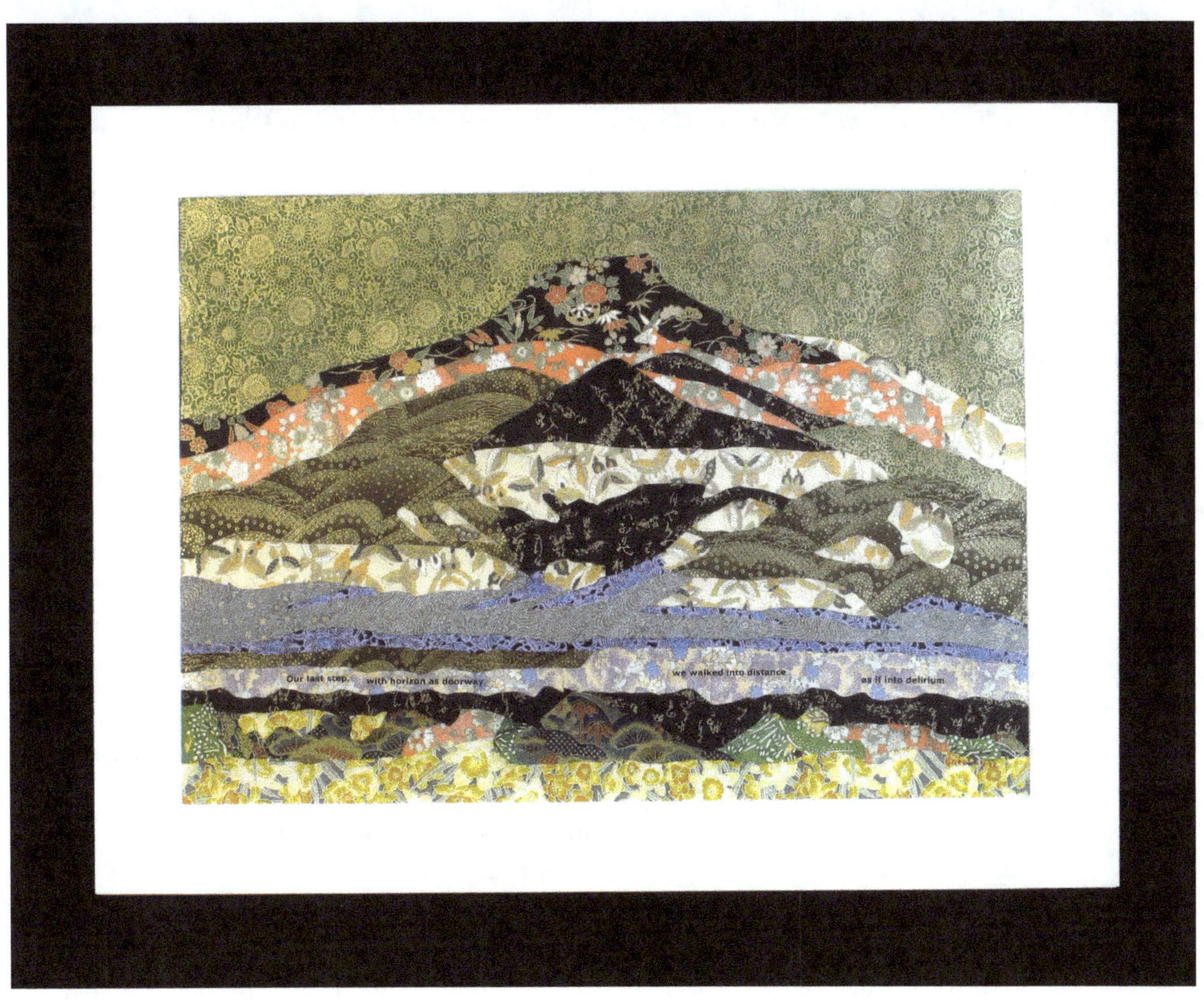

Charles Greeley, "The Mesa the Shadow Built," Japanese paper collage, 18 x 24"

Daughters in Winter

Michelle Holland

"Every moment is a moment of grace, every hour an offering. . . ."—Elie Wiesel

The geraniums on the south window sill
bloom bright pink against slate grey clouds
and the crystal surface of white snow.
When night falls, the snow will continue to rest
on the juniper branches outside my window.
I split and stacked a dead woman's piñon and cedar,
and built the fires in our house to protect us from this cold season.
In the light of a full December moon,
the shadows grow long and shape shift until
out of the corner of my eye I see a chariot,
driven by a dark form who threatens to steal all that I love.
Demeter refused to grant a growing season until her daughter was returned.
I would easily cast the world into an eternity of ice,
or heave the earth up into mountains for each of my own two daughters.

I wish to gather armies, divert them from burning down nations.
Help me raise my daughters, give them horses with armor,
a red flag flapping, and the beat of victory drums.
Give them the power of weapons of mass destruction
to take in their innocent hands and crush them
into gardens, communities, families that will never see their children enter battle.

But, I am small. No goddess runs in my blood.
The moon only an orb of unattainable beauty,
rises too large, just beyond my reach.
Gravity bound and thin-skinned, all the courage I have rides in the pulse
I so blindly felt when I held their infant heads against the palm of my hand.
A sweet blue vein under their fuzzy blond hair,
a fragile circuit transported all they could be.
I am small, so entirely mortal that the protection I raise
is only as fierce as my voice can muster.

Daughters of flesh and blood, they whirl their dreams
each night a dance of recipes, romances, new homes, soccer games,
the pound of their feet around the curves of high school tracks,
the angles of geometry, the balance of scientific equations,
the last customer's drink order, the hours in a day.
They have been as safe as the geraniums on the window sill,
assured in their blossoming that spring will arrive.

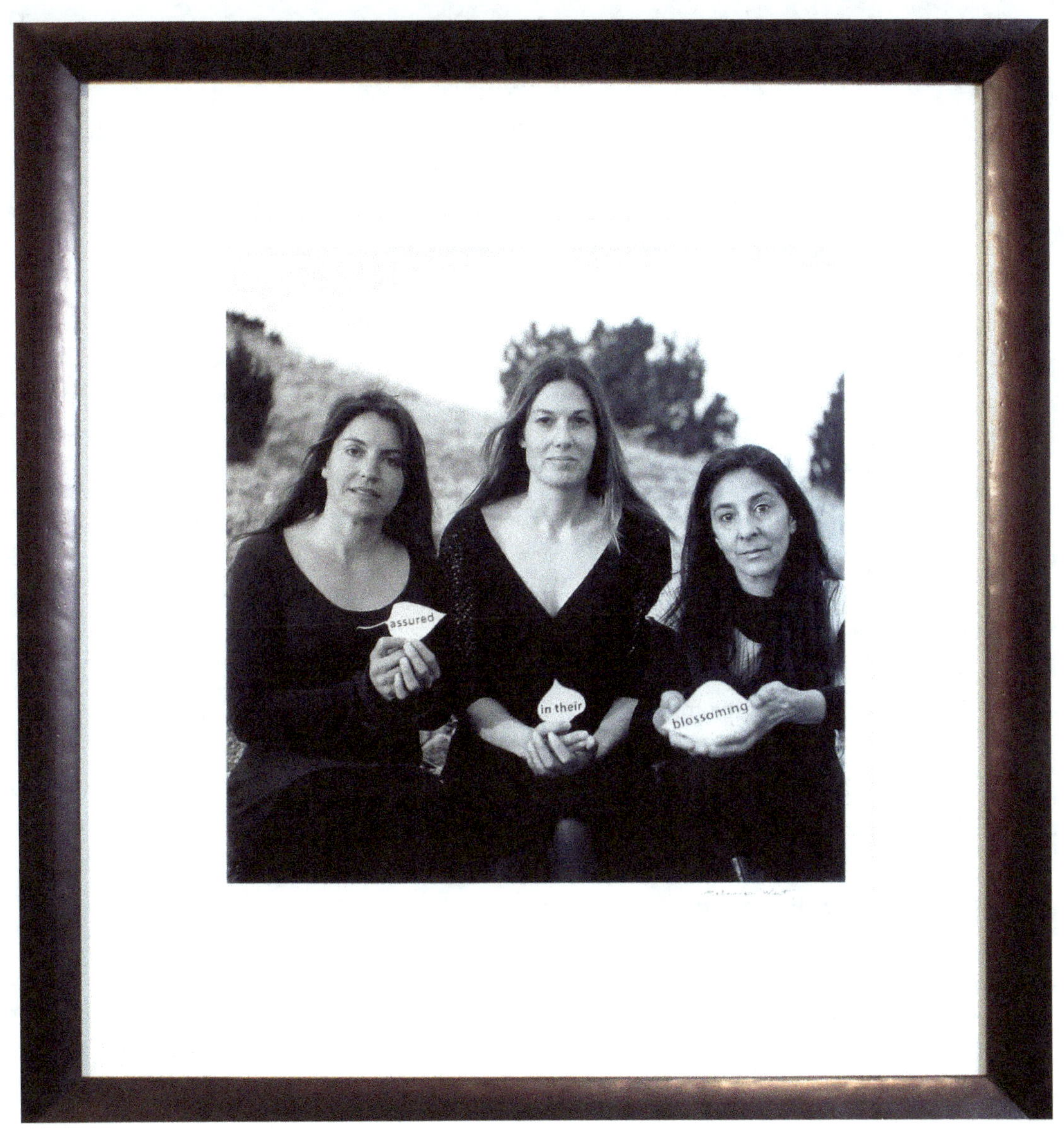

Melanie West, "Lucy, Kelcey and Eva," digital C print, 24 x 25"

On Lynn's Porch, 7 11 11
Kathamann

Indian ink water washes a monsoon
    sky heavy with rain.
Dragonflies chaotic in air heat.
    Is it raining at my house?
Biscuit whacks Ellie with her tail.
    We lose the sun
The ink clouds bleed like capillary
    action on rice paper.

Aunt Caroline succumbs to
    morphine and leukemia.
Her graciousness filled with internal
    bleeding.
Bite-size maroon cherries ripe for
    picking.
First scent of moisture in the cool
    breeze. My nostrils celebrate.

Mount Vertebra awaiting deluge
    Trees turn under leaves upwards.
Cherry pits and stems segregated to
    one bowl side.
Rumbling skies in a wet atmosphere.
    Summer peace in the high desert.

Small dust jumps at each rain drop.
    We will survive the season
with rainy afternoon storms.
    Air thick like a wet dog.
Turquoise veins of rain and forehead
    furrows of arroyos.
394 drops, then stops.
    Ghostly white curtains of
walking rain creeping towards us.

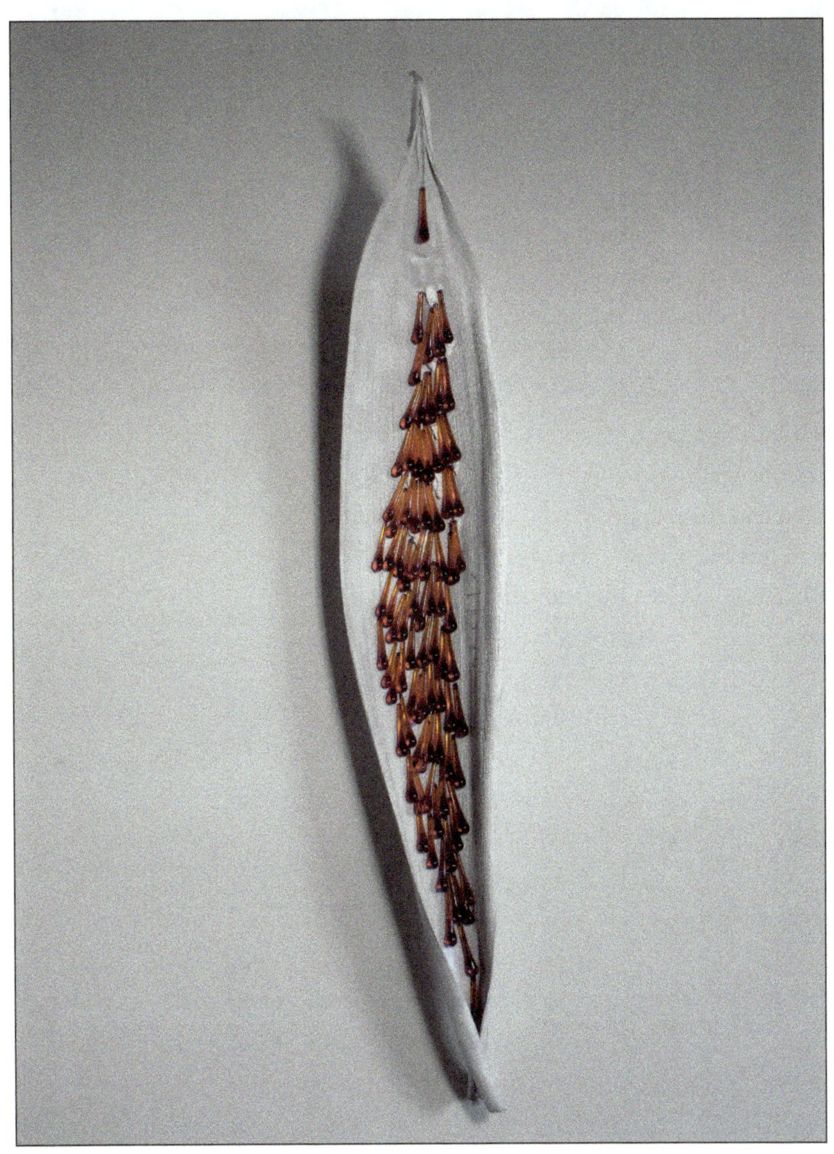

Shirley Klinghoffer, "Vessel II," unique seed pod and glass, 50 x 10 x 3"

Sleeping Beauties
Piper Leigh

is the name cartographers give blank spaces.
Spring runoff from the Sangres fills the river.
Geese return. The world warms up.
You push and pull oars, use the current
for navigation, take in stone's quiet,
sleep deeply on grassy shelves.
I follow you into the gorge.
An explorer, you leave
the excavated and the mapped,
content with this red-yellow curve,
sandstone passage between this moment
and the next.

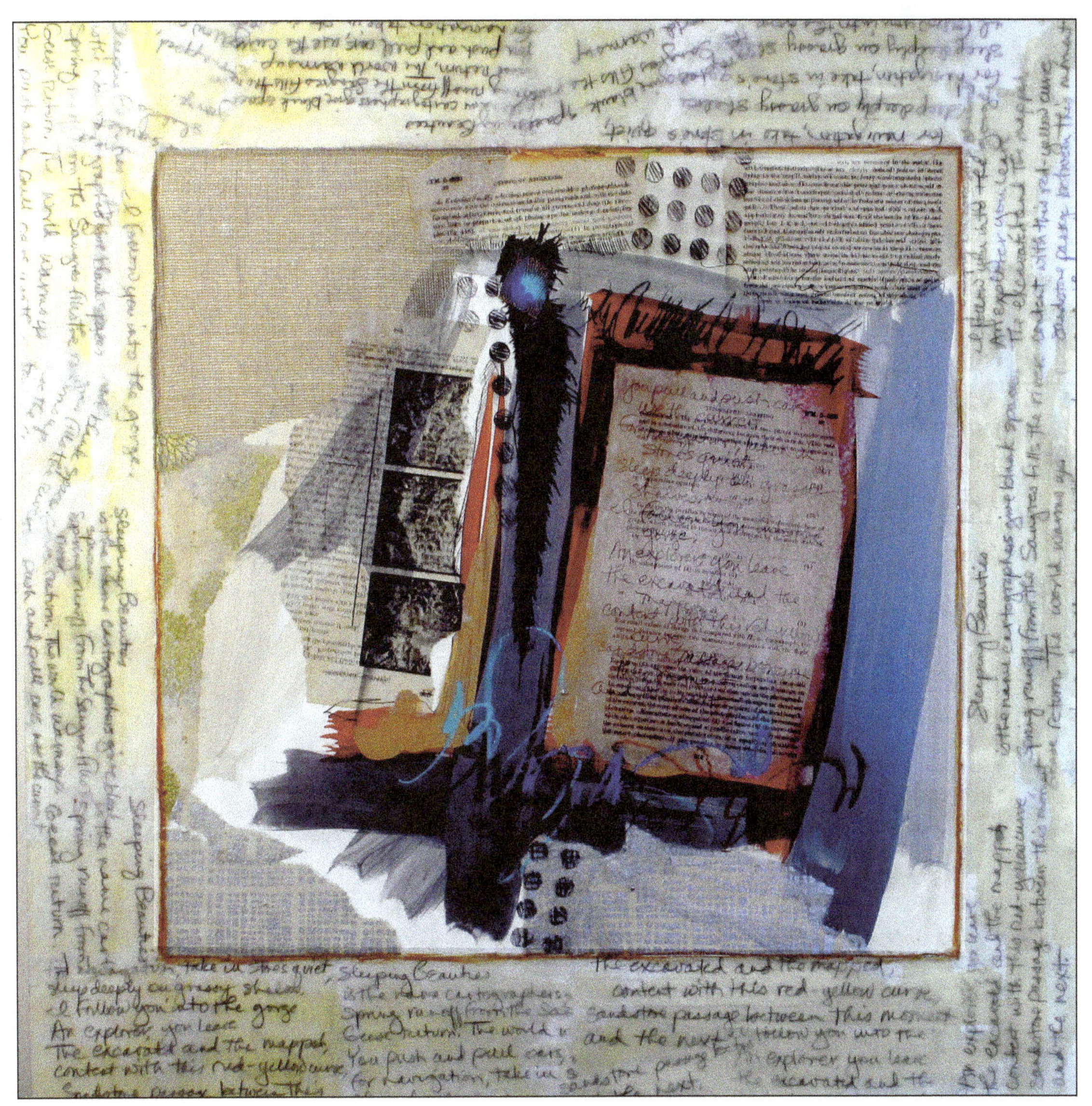

Sallyann Paschall, "Verbal Structure," mixed media, 24 x 24 x 2"

The Geese at Bosque Del Apache
Donald Levering

As god of destruction, Shiva holds in one hand a flame which burns away the veil of time and opens our minds to eternity.

——Joseph Campbell

What is the signal before
seventeen thousand four hundred eleven snow geese
quiet their raucous murmur

and lift from the lake in a whirlwind,
angling toward the horizon, veering
back overhead, casting their shadow

selves across the land and water
one full round, resettling on the surface
to resume their ruckus?

Where did they take me
when the net of their shadows passed over
like accelerated film telescoping time,

all my life's shades and sunshine flashing
in submission to the single purpose of geese?
Was each of their black-tipped wings

a healing hand, or limb of dancing Shiva,
my pain and bliss but ash
from the flame revealed

in the rush of white feathers?

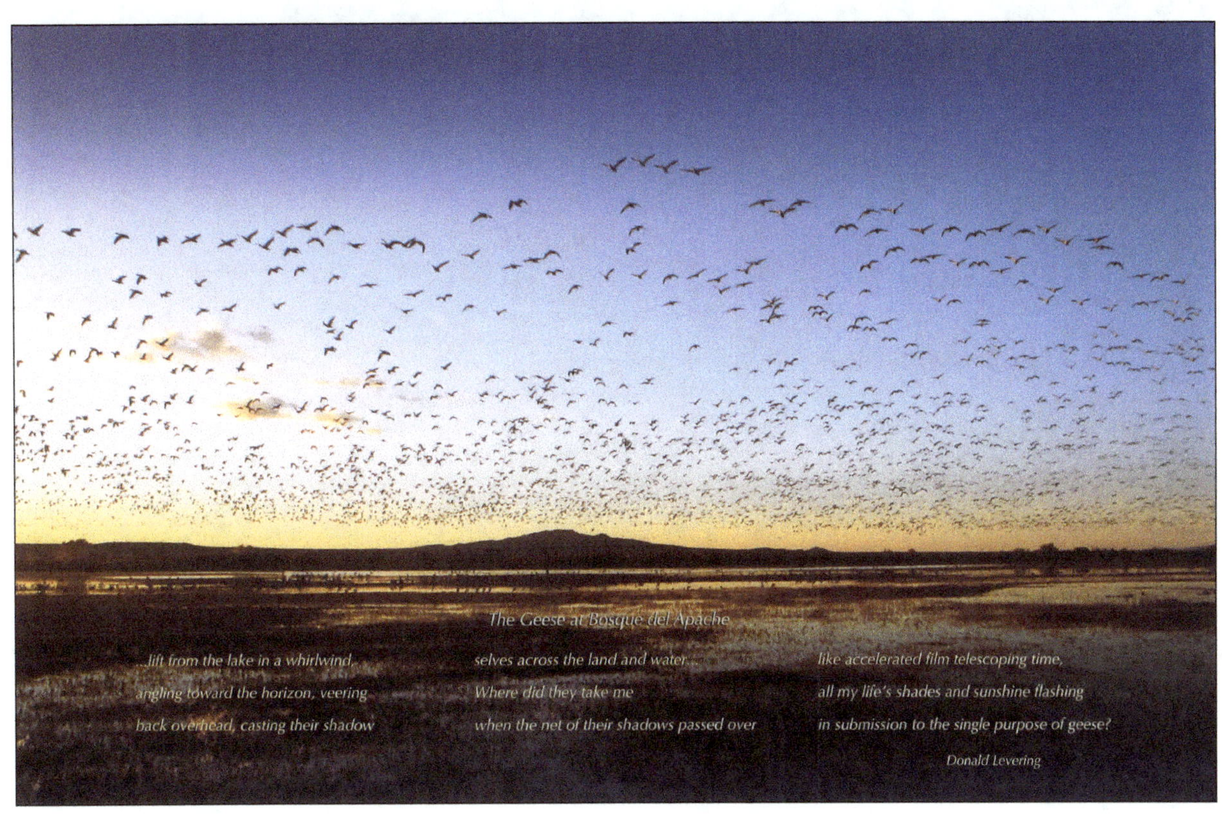

Cynthia West, "The Geese at Bosque Del Apache," photograph, 21 x 28"

Pure Land
Dana Levin

    Shedding-So-Glorious—
Buddha
    Of the autumn djinns—

    His consort, Golden-
Sensation—

    You'd brushed by chamisa. A
honey-palaced air—

    As if a smell
could be a place, musk-heavy and gold,
    a glorious
Pure
    Land—

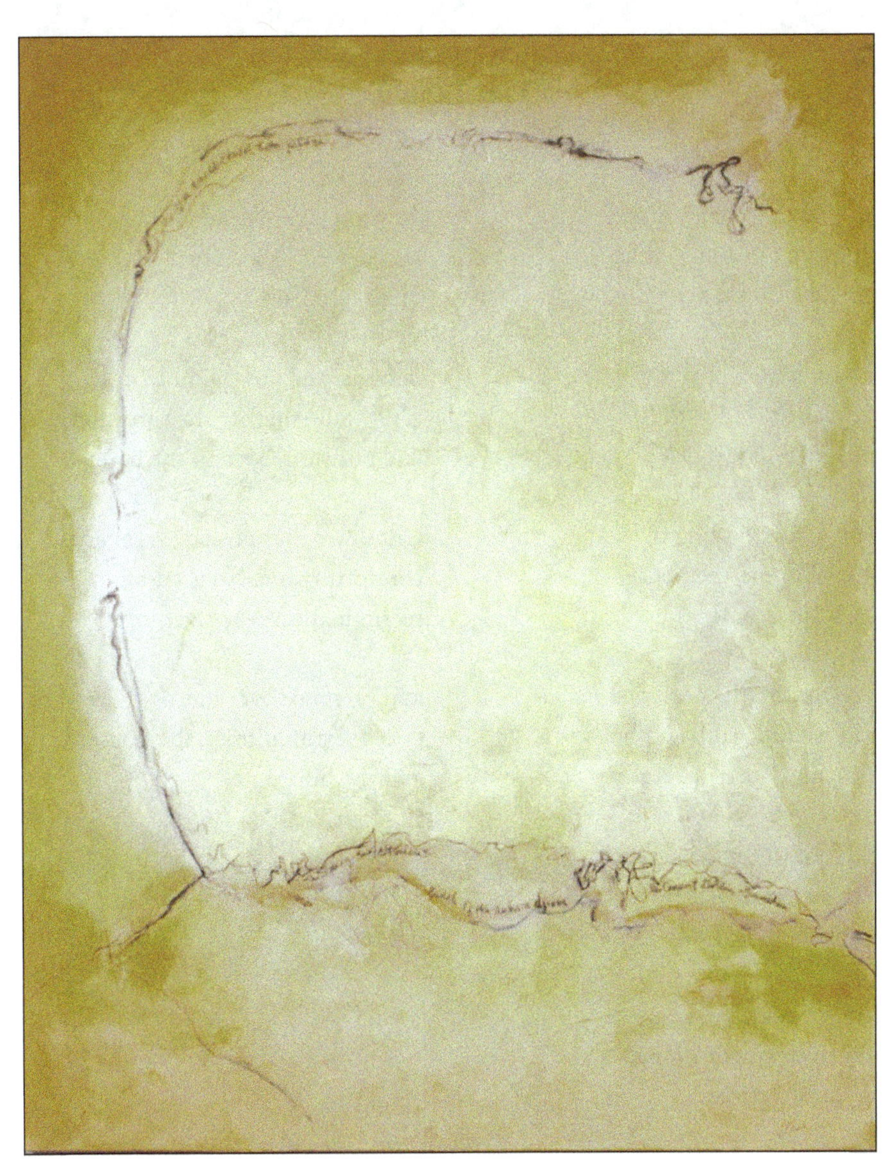

Ann Laser, "Golden Sensation," acrylic, 60 x 48"

Requiem
Jane Lipman

The great-grandmother juniper
didn't complain as I touched her
great, soft-needled branches

and said goodbye.
Eighteen years I lived with her.
She came down so fast.

What have I done, letting my fear
of fire, fear of losing the house,
fear of firescapers' omens

give the cut order. She preceded me,
blessed this setting, land and house
long before me. For two decades

I watched birds flit in her branches
through the seasons. Beheld
heavy snow bow her down

to the ground in a way she never
stood fully up again, brushing,
caressing me as I passed.

In strong winds and storms
she heaved recklessly.
Held her place

between the bow windows.
Grew tall—higher than the house
and outward, beyond the path.

Cut down, her presence remains,
comforting me. No accusation,
recrimination—just her love

and presence over me, over the birds,
over the piñon trees, the house
and the hill.

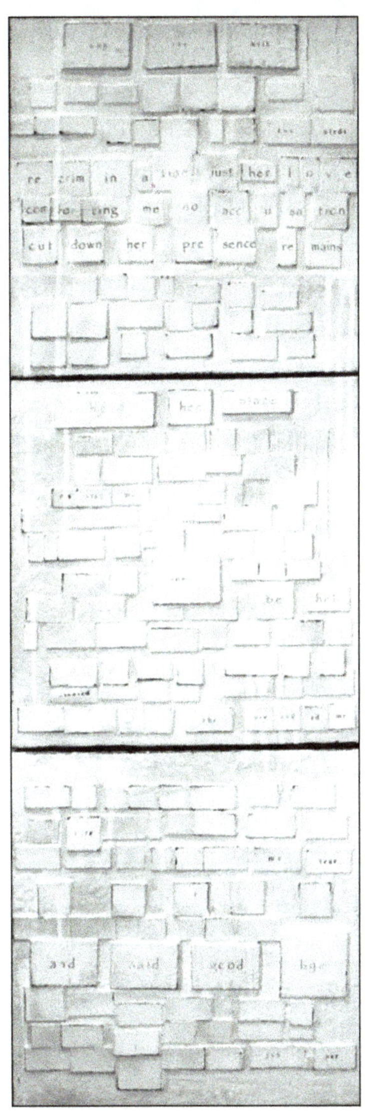

Blair Vaughn-Gruler, “Just Her Love,” oil/balsa wood/cardboard and letters on canvas and panel, 48 x 16 x 1.5”

Unpunctuated Awe
Joan Logghe

for WS Merwin

So beautiful today
I don't know what to do with it
I can't be outside it's too perfect
the morning glories are too too without
even ingesting their known iota of trip
The Maximillian sunflowers are poised
to bloom and even that potential is wildly
enticing into too beautiful The dues we paid
After the fires after the wind and smoke the terrible
canyon fires of Santa Clara watershed tears shed
I could cry again today for the world we earned
paid its dues to too beautiful too beautiful
beautiful datura beautiful the Jewish New Year
I am already lamenting I stand naked for an hour
in my greenhouse watching the cereus flower
prepare for night blooming I stand naked before
my shower and after my shower another phone call
from the too beautiful I talk naked on the phone
because I don't know how to manage today
with how I love too beautiful the note in the mail
from you how I love poets and painters who make
the world shine me I never want to set foot
inside a classroom with no windows
I want to speak poetry to those finches
and to the kale I will tell the kale I forgive the aphids
you are so greenly beautiful I love my body today
because it is the vessel that carried too beautiful
soon departing for other beauty don't mention
it you say but in the too beautiful death
is already sharpening its scythe on too beautiful
its harvest of basil scent and mint too many
tomatoes and a glut of cucumbers and I forget
that I know how to preserve   I am doing it now

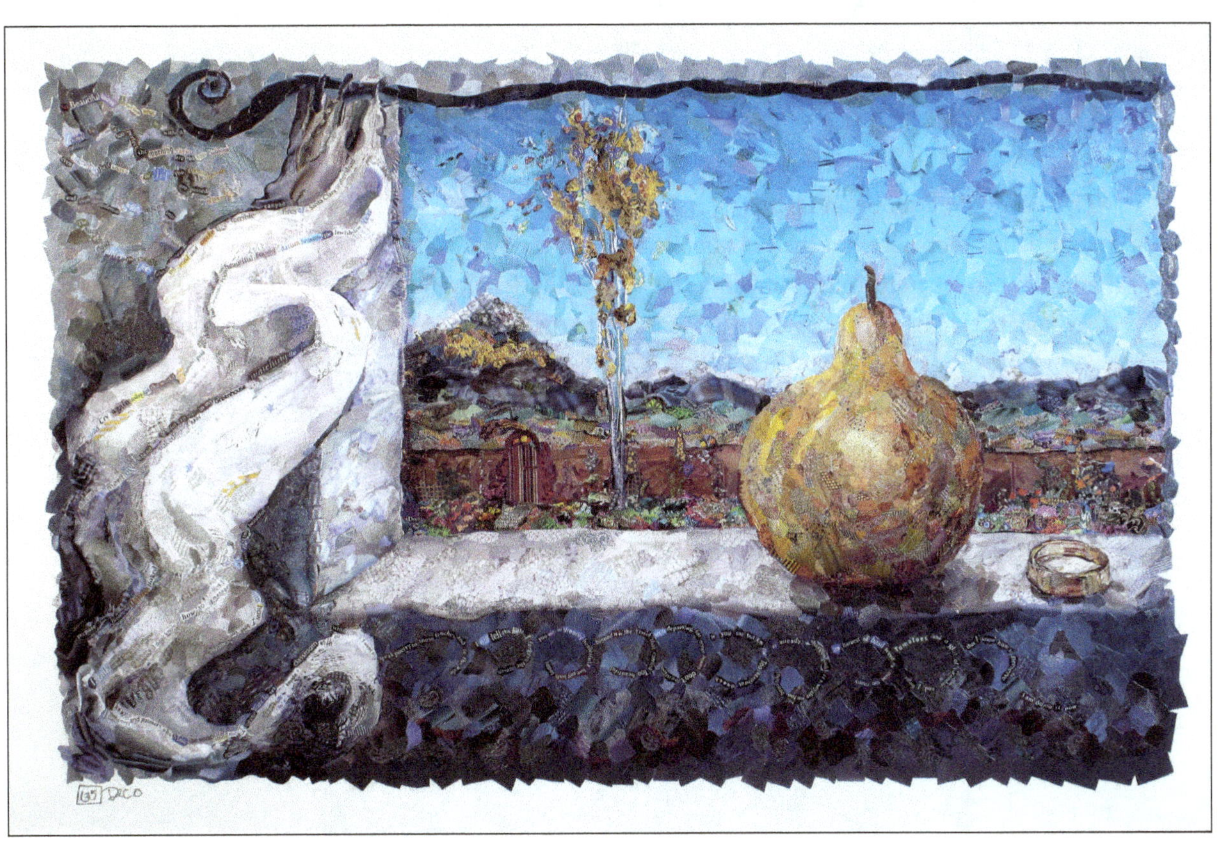

Bernadette Freeman, “Small Window,” paper assemblage, 28 x 18”

Wild Pears

Mary McGinnis

wild in sunlight knobby and hard
in our hands they fall from the trees barely touched they are
lumpy and sweet sunwarmed, smelling like wine underfoot we walk on
disconnected stems our feet pressing ripeness into dirt we

pick in Galisteo village quietness taking
enough to fill your hat taking some from every tree they
are a strange taste on my tongue
as rough and pungent as my
smallest longing

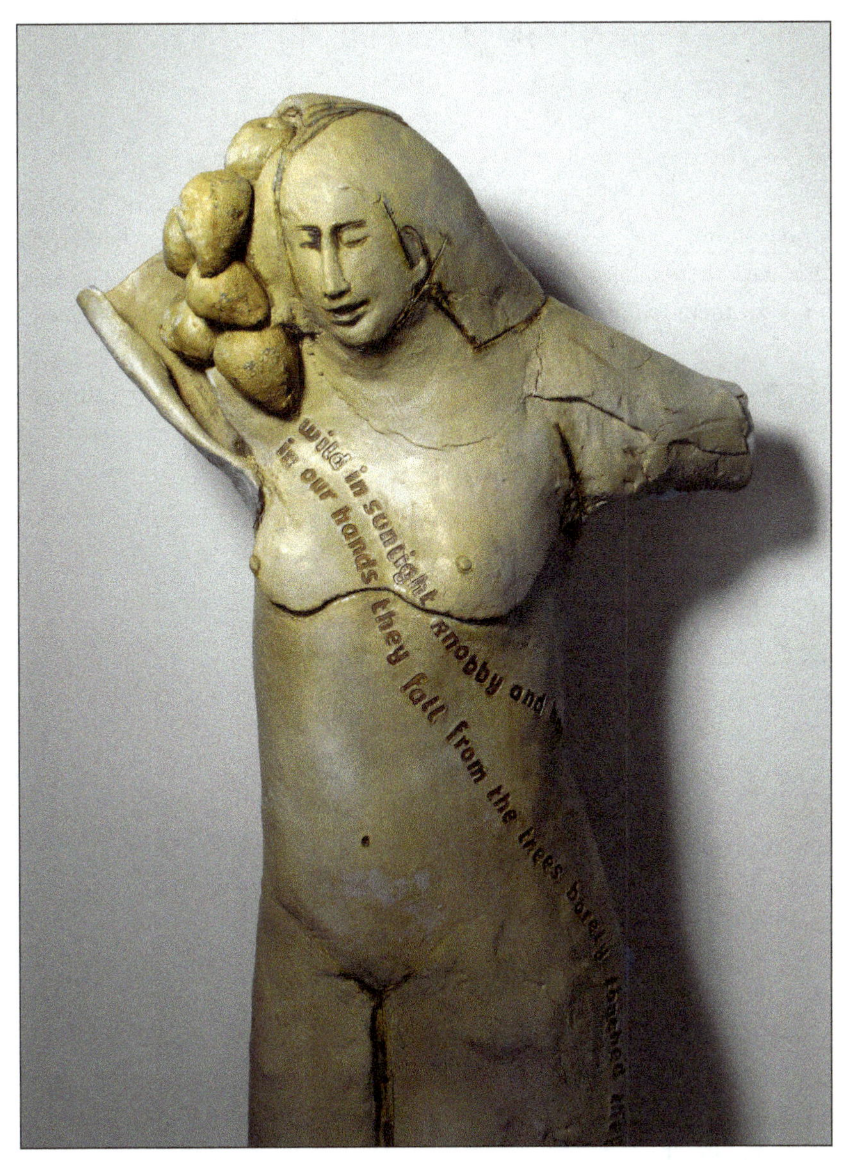

Ruth Weston, “Wild Pears,” clay and stone, 48 x 24 x 20”

The Archeologist as Full Moon

James McGrath

for Kurt Anschultz

Like a full moon,
he smiled at three figures
carved on stone, gave them names.
Was he listening for them to give him his name?

He stared at a hunter eyeing a delicate deer
carved on stone,
traced their lines with an artist's eye.
Was he imagining the hunter hunting him?

He paused, squinted at carved panels of spears,
birds impaled on some.
Was he noting how the spears pointed
up at the stars?

He knelt down to capture the bird on a stalk of corn
carved on stone.
Was he hearing the rustle of cornstalks
in the valley below?
Was he hearing the last song of that bird
before it became stone?

He searched for carved corn, gardens or fields.
Was he feeling his own hunger for the earth?
Did he dream of sinking his feet into mud,
or pressing his hand into clay
to make a bowl for his laughter and tears?

And those shields carved on stone,
was he feeling safe when he photographed them?
Did he reach for his own shield
when he saw clouds sheltering the mountain?

I watched him stepping about those carved stones.
He left nothing behind.

I wanted the flute player to bring him home,
a full moon.

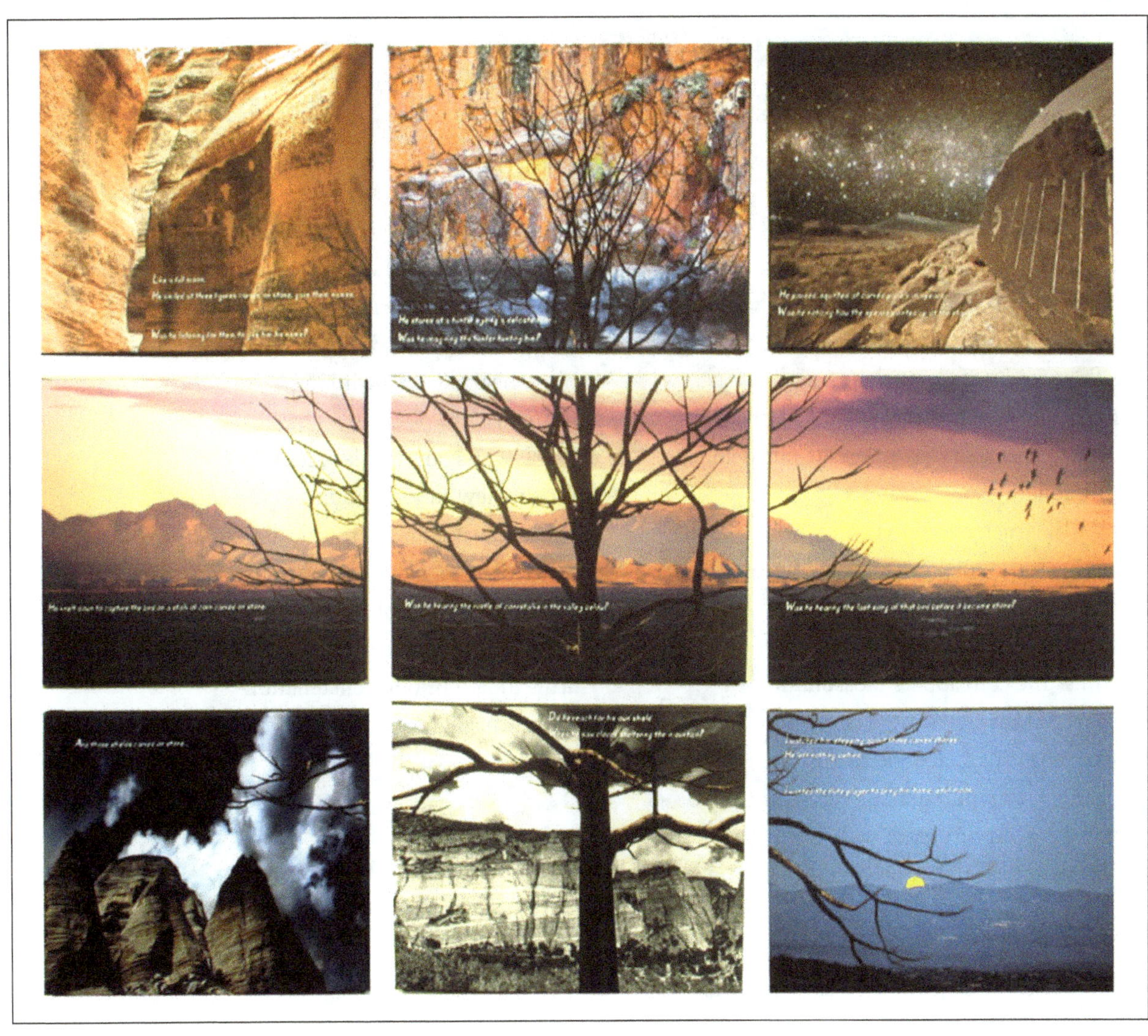

S.K. Yeatts, "The Archaeologist as Full Moon," giclee photography on stretched canvas, 58 x 47"

Our New Life
Carol Moldaw

If the field is thick
with horse shit and the garden
unplanted, and the roof
needs repair; if after the next storm
sand from the acequia
overflows and suffocates the marsh,
killing the cattails where redwinged blackbirds nest,
if the neighbors' horses overgraze our field,
if I am lonely,
if a WIPP truck overturns
going back and forth from Los Alamos
to the shifting salt pits in Carlsbad,
if we go away for a week
and miss the crab apple's blossoming,
the sheep shearing,
if it turns out I am allergic to Russian olives,
to chamisa, to rabbit grass,
if they pave our dirt road,
if the cat returns to her original owner,
if the walls need remudding after every storm,
if the doctor finds a problem,
if the beer cans and corn chip bags and whiskey bottles
pile up on the road
faster than we can collect them for the dump,
if the doctor doesn't know what is wrong,
if Los Alamos gets the contract
to manufacture or stockpile or do anything whatever
with nuclear warheads,
if I cut my foot on a rusty washing machine part
while walking down by the river,
if I get lost in the Barrancas,
if my heart keeps shrinking,
if my heart explodes–
will I ever again think to look
for the new moon's thinnest crescent,
will we ever crane our necks together,
as we used to, name the stars,
turn down the cool sheets,
go to bed not exhausted,
arms linked in one constellation
that turns all night in sync with the sky?

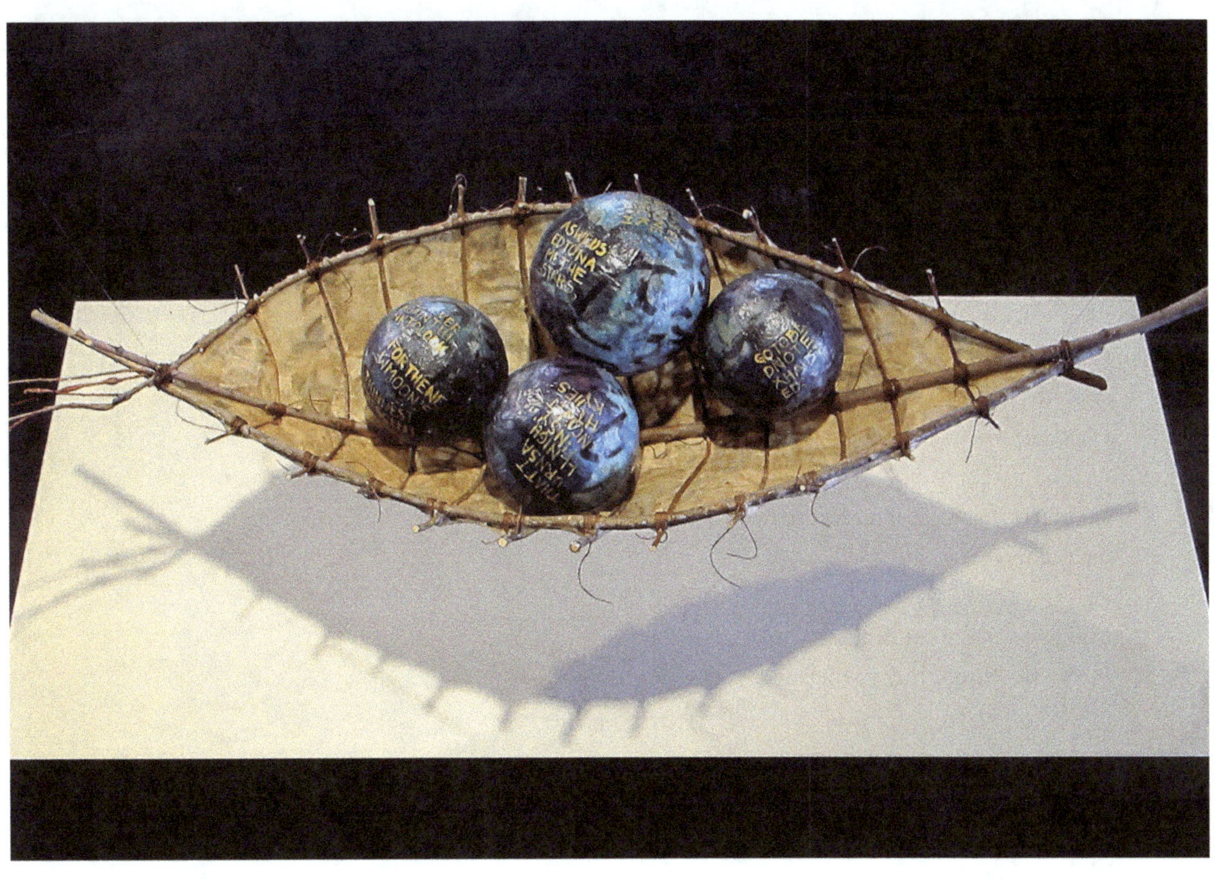

Julie Wagner, "RN.WL.F," ink on paper/sticks/glue, 10 x 4 x 46"

Acupuncture with Dr. Hao
Mary Morris

There are ninety-seven points in the ear.

Three women on the bank sip tea
from celadon green cups.

A quartet plays something exquisite.
He takes my pulse

as though feeling for a forgotten road
on a map within my body.

I lie in a mist of tenderness.
He works through deep meridians

in the landscape of my interior.
He is thinking spleen, lung.

My eyes are closed.
I am in Guangzhou.

He is connecting points,
in anatomical constellations.

The *Qui River* opens beyond
the emerald bamboo forest.

I am on a boat in the channel
of the immortals

as Dr. Hao rows
quietly into the future
for a cure.

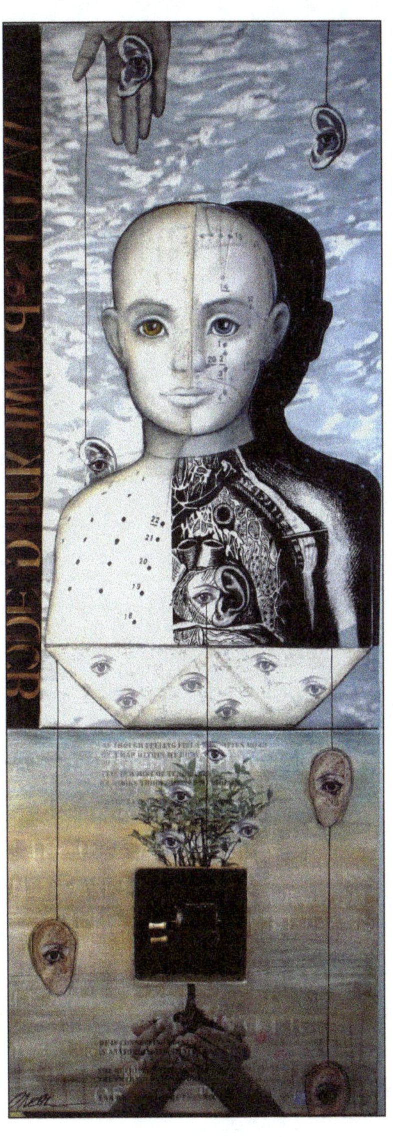

Janet O'Neal, "Landscape of the Interior," assemblage of acrylics/collage/photography/pencil and found objects on wood and canvas, 20 x 56 x 3"

At the Wheel of the Year
Elizabeth Raby

The leg scratch of crickets sounds
from drying sage. Thunder rolls
from white clouds out of the west.
Wind on her summer burnt arms
is a soft stroking, neither warm nor cool.
This is the time of the singing moon.

One angry skrank of a jay.
In uncharacteristic silence,
a chickadee eats seed. Day-lily
leaves yellow, dry seed stalks
rattle, burrs wait for the unwary.

Orange butterflies have curled their tongues
back from rich purple blossoms of buddleia,
sit on pink sandstone, open and close their wings—
Satiation? Thanksgiving? Farewell? They rest.
At a signal in butterfly they rise together
into the breeze, beat their way back
to their purple banquet.

All around is abundance, bloom, seed,
sun and breeze, cloud and sky,
mountain and green meadow,
orange zinnia, purple aster, yellow goldenrod.
Larvae wriggle in the watery hollow of a rock.
The world does sing, then holds its breath
in the final moment before the cold comes down.

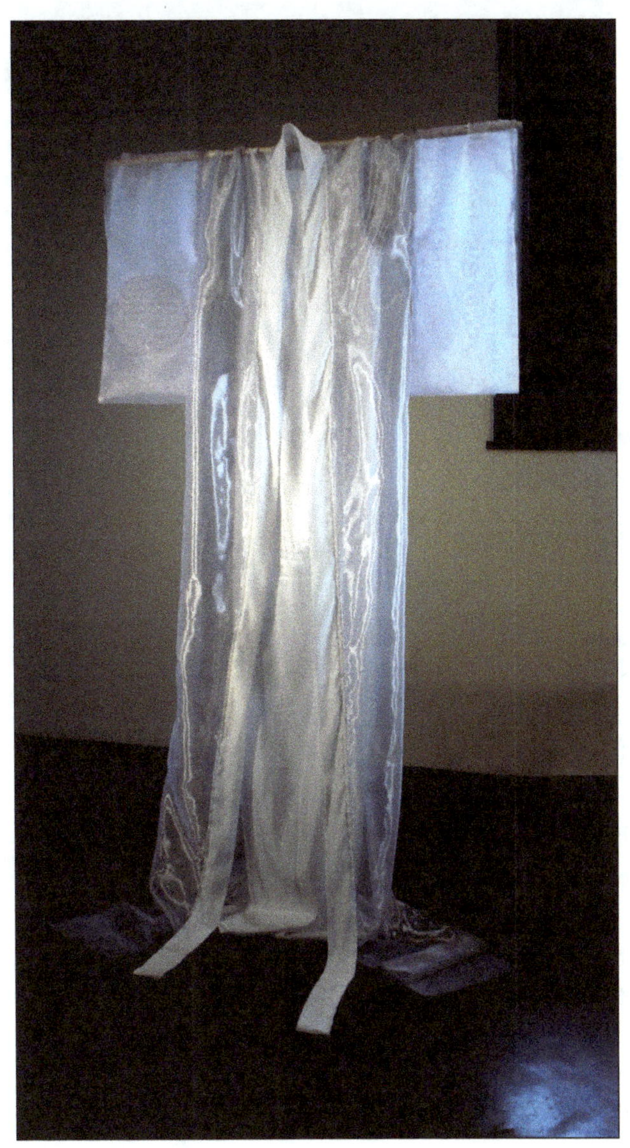

Piper Leigh, “Singing Moon,” cloth, 7 x 3’

The Moon Speaks of Santa Fe

Stella Reed

You, broken poem of brown stucco,
rough rhyme of adobe wall
your fingers smell like sage.
Feel the red stone at the center of your belly,
it has always been there.
You genuflect at the altar of art
the back of your knees hide memories
of turquoise and horse hair,
the braid of DeVargas lengthens your spine
but your tongue is Tewa.

Oh City of Mud with your
scarcity of water, paucity of bugs,
your river bed a sacrament,
you are flat-roofed, even tempered,
Zo-zoed and Meemed;
baptized in chile, bottle-fed on blood,
the sap of the pinon runs in your veins.

Creature Different, City Beautiful,
La Villa Real of Holy Fe,
before sunlight folds the datura
let my light cast one more glance
on your Blood of Christ Mountains.
See there, the Virgin in her mantle of stars
spills roses at the feet of your faith.

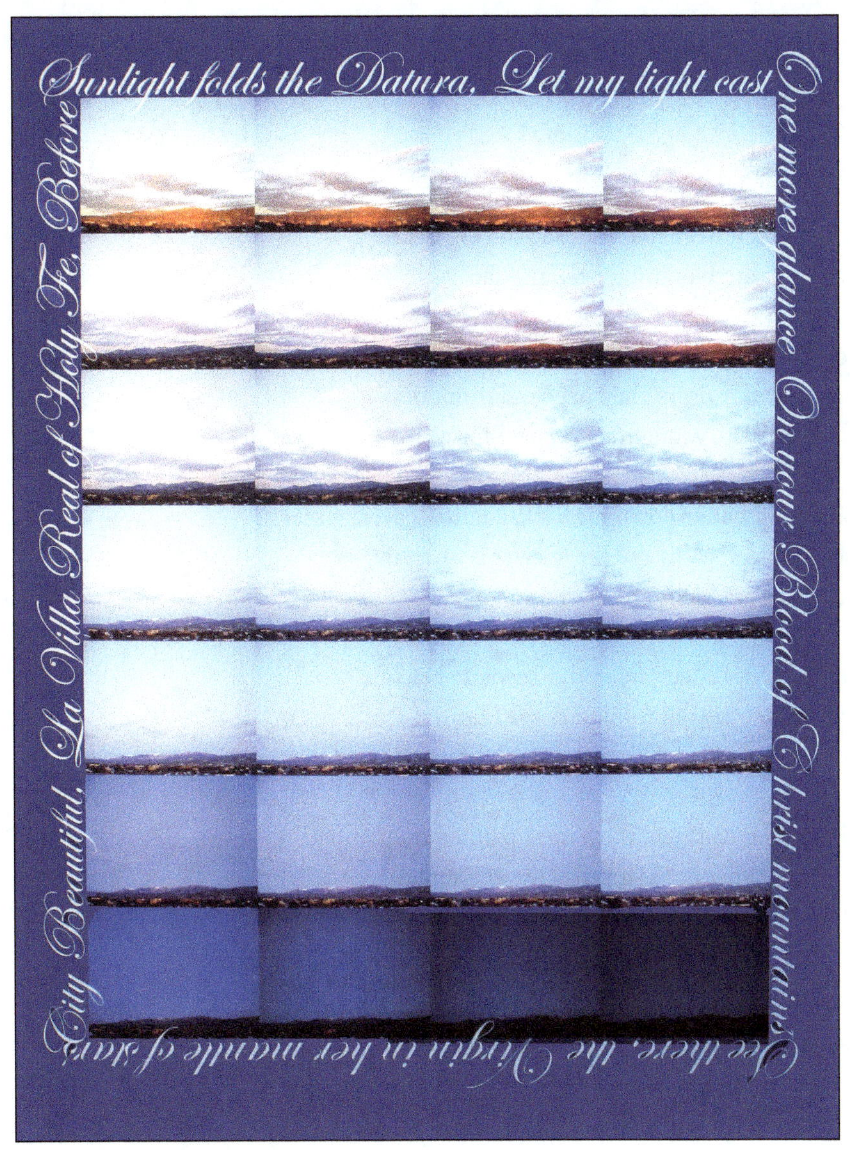

Carol Sky, "City Beautiful," archival pigment print on canvas, 42 x 32"

VILLANELLE
Barbara Robidoux

In barrio de Analco young men prepare for war
"Don't Go!" an old woman cries "You are too dear!"
Roses, red roses are blooming near and far

The moon hangs full, you cannot see a star
at the shrine of the virgin they pray and drink beer
In barrio de Analco, young men prepare for war

Juan's long braid hangs down his back, a tattoo covers a scar
He asks the others "Why go" the answer is unclear
Roses, red roses are blooming near and far

"Let's go!" he yells "Meet me at the Tecolote bar."
the others follow, the old woman doesn't hear
In barrio de Analco, young men prepare for war

The night surrounds them, the Virgin painted on their car
The old woman fingers her rosary, now she shows her fear
Roses, red roses are blooming near and far

A candle burns. Old woman's door is left ajar
Moonlight enters now the ghosts appear
In barrio de Analco young men prepare for war
Roses, red roses are blooming, near and far

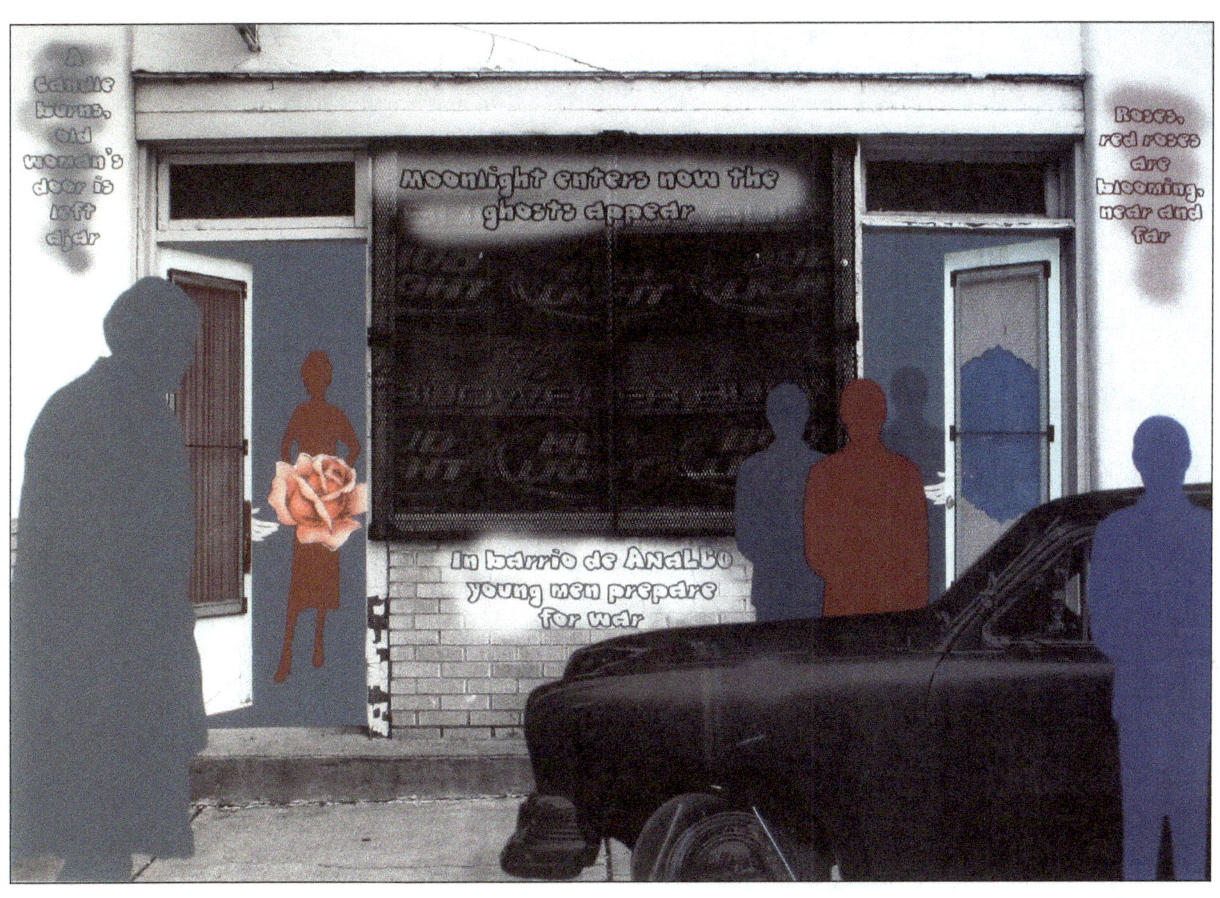

Michael Stone, "Welcome," digital collage, 36 x 24"

Letter from Georgia O'Keeffe To Alfred Stieglitz Upon Seeing His Photograph Of Her Hands

Barbara Rockman

Be calm, Alfred. No,
I am a plain woman. I rinse dishes,
pull weeds and unleash the dogs on dirt trails.
I sleep in a narrow bed. I rise early.
These are hands that mix paint,
decipher sky. With these hands
I scratch my head at the improbable.
I twist them under my breasts in sleep.
Fisted against my stomach they fly
from my body in dream. Hands
at the tips of wings, Alfred.
How you splayed my fingers,
insisted I caress the absent forelock,
empty sockets, each stone molar,
imagining the horse's rough tongue.
I want nothing of death, Alfred, nothing
of absence. These elegant hands cup seeds,
cut back Echinacea, snip herbs for the sauce.
They tug knotted shirts from a basket, shake them
into light, clamp them to the line with bleached pins.
What can a man know of a woman's hands?

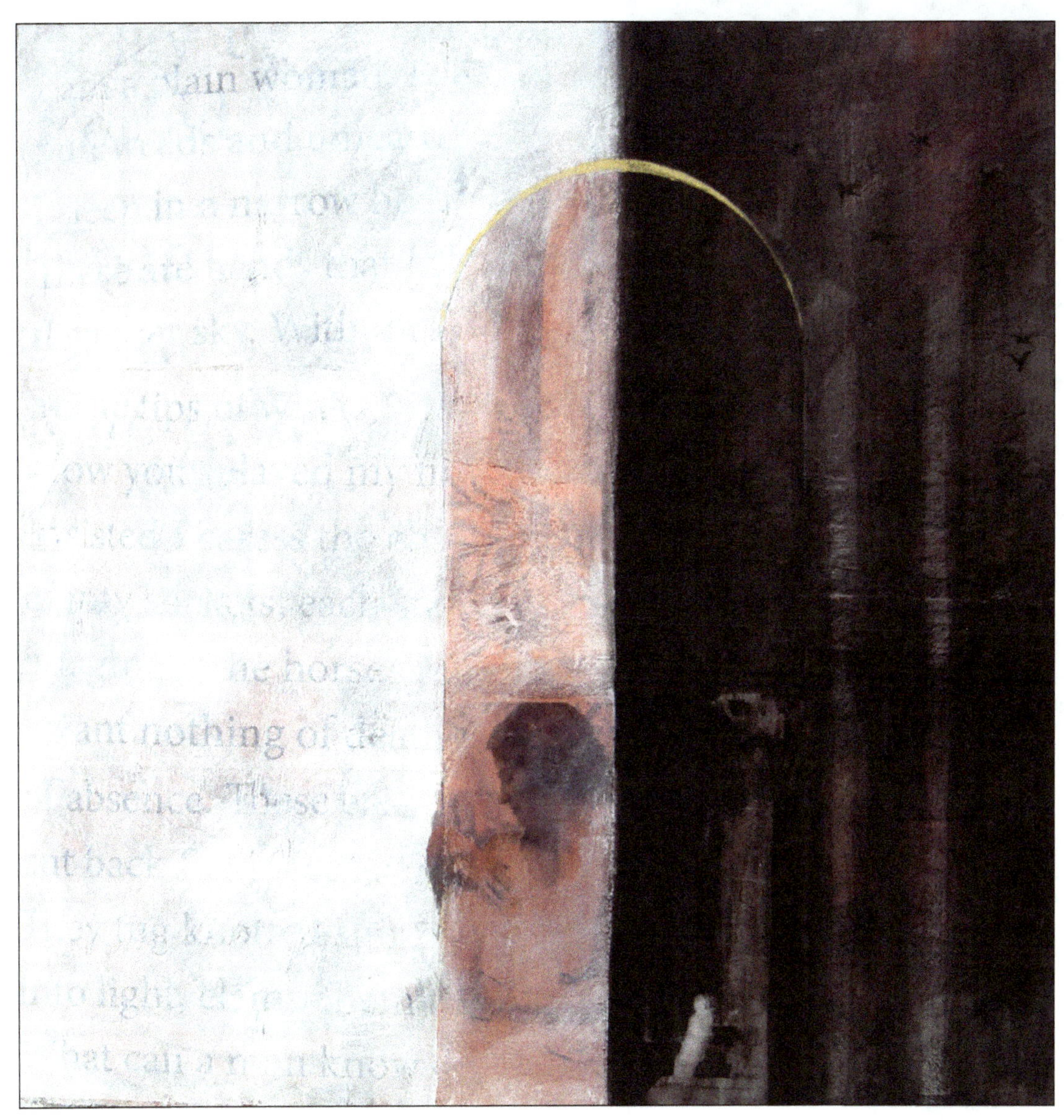

Dawn Chandler, “I Am a Plain Woman,” mixed media on panel, 24 x 24”

Una Canción de Flores
Leo Romero

Listen to Celso
and you'd think anything was possible

Celso claims the moon is a woman
who carries a large knife
he has seen her cut down stars
which came too close

    Anoche la luna
    salió de los arboles
    con un cuchillo largo

    La luna tiene cabello blanco
    ojos blancos
    labios blancos

Celso has heard the moon sing
songs of flowers

Celso carries a long knife
to be like the moon
he tells everyone he is in love
and brandishes the knife gently
as if he were beheading roses

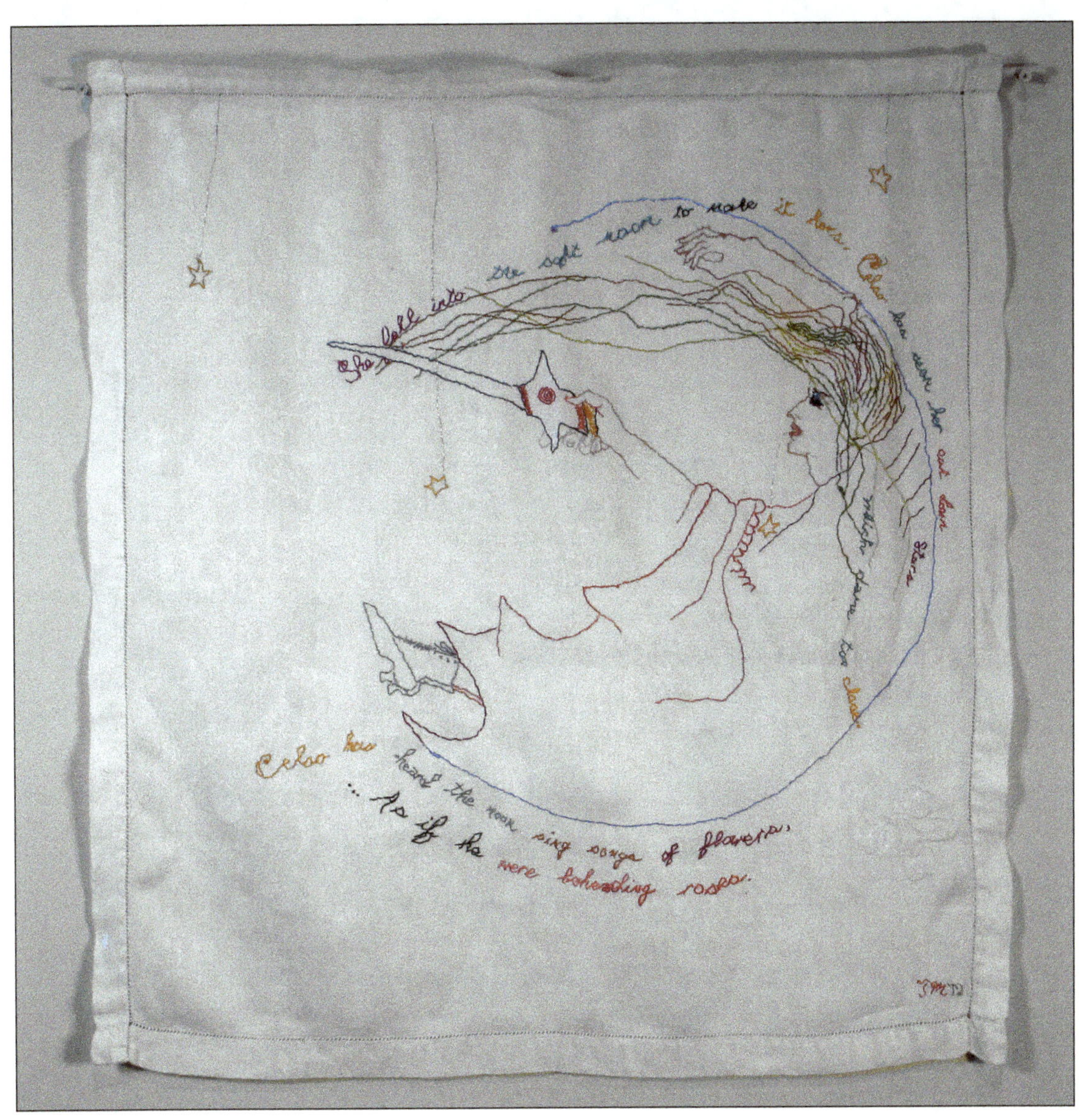

Thelma Mathias, "Una Cancion des Estrellas," embroidery thread on linen, 25 x 24"

Juxtaposition
Levi Romero

throughout the years I have designed
high-end custom homes
crafting spatial poetics with *vigas* and *latillas*
hand peeled by *mojados*
whose sweat translates into profit for developers
working at a nifty rate

sometimes I go visit these homes
as they are being finished

"may I help you? "
I am asked by the realtor
standing at the door,
thinking that I may be the guy
who mixed the mud and pushed the wheel barrow

I introduce myself as the designer

"oh, well, it's so nice to meet you,
what a wonderful job!
please, come in."

I once was asked by a home magazine journalist
if I felt insulted by such incidents
" well, no," I said, my mind mixing for an answer
"a good batch of cement is never accidental "

last year on my way up through Santa Fe
I made a detour and drove by a house of my design

the season's first snow on the ground,
smoke rising out of the fireplace chimney

inch by inch
I know that house
through its X,Y and Z axis

but, I cannot approach the front door
knock and expect to be invited in
to sit in the corner of my pleasing
and lounge around with the owner
as we sip on cups of hot herbal tea
making small talk about the weather

or discussing a reading
by the latest author come through
as the sun's last light
streams in gallantly
through the window
just where I placed it
and for that reason

I take a handful of snow to my mouth
toss another into the air
my blessing upon the inhabitants
"que Dios los bendiga y les de mas"
my grandfather would have said

I turn my car toward home
to my mother's house
a place near and far to me

she, my mother, is bedridden
and my brother is the self appointed caretaker
to bathe her and feed her
bring her morsels of conversation

it is their own world now

ruled by a juxtaposition of understanding
against what I have come to know, now
here, so far and away

I am greeted at her front yard
by an old, propped up, truck hood
proclaiming my brother's spray-painted inscription
Jesus Saves
on the opposite side it reads
Keep Out!

"I guess it just depends on
what kind of day he's having,"
someone once remarked
like a rattle snake
it's a fair warning

years ago I accepted this madness
and called it not my own
"it's better that he be drunk on Christ," said my mother
"than on what he used to drink "

we all agreed

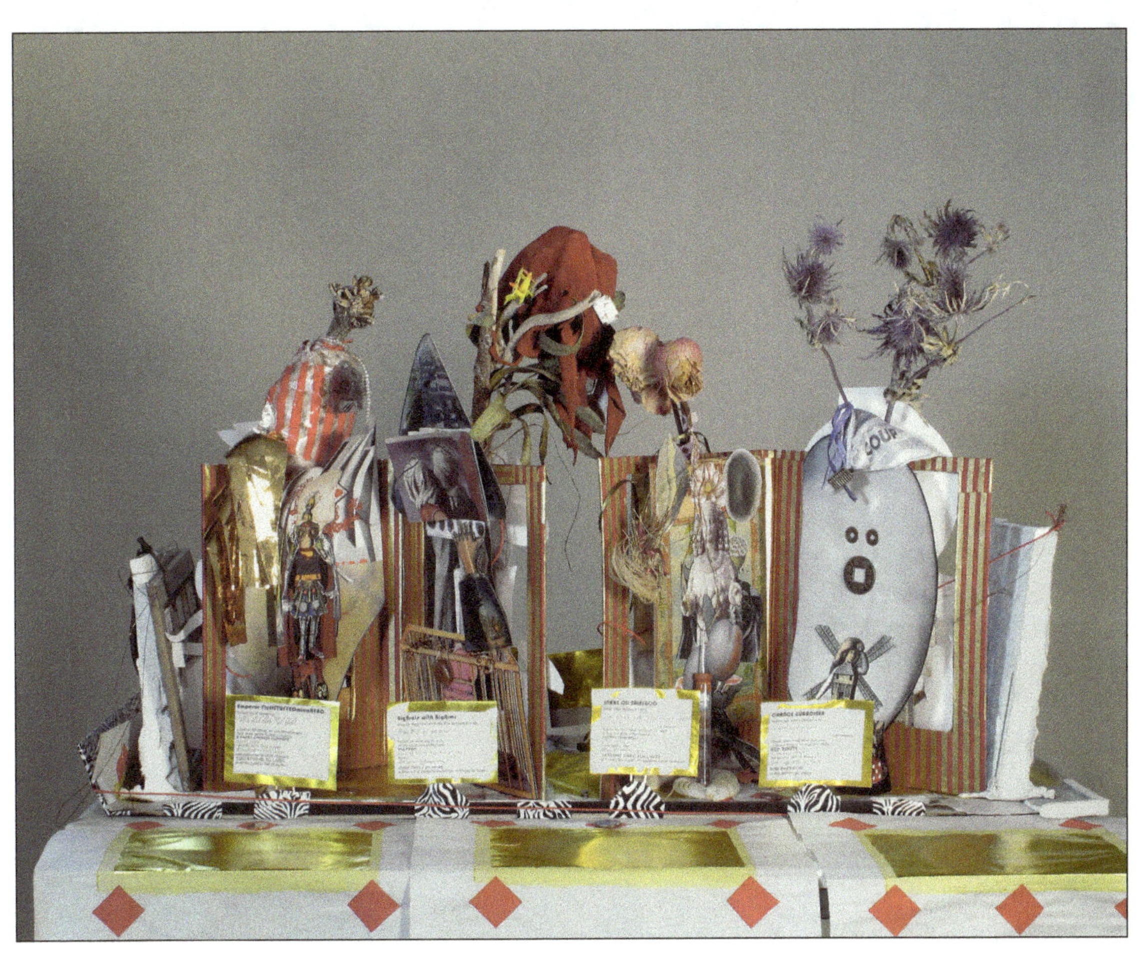

Suzanne Vilmain, "A Book Sculpture Homage to Scarecrows," mixed media, 3 x 2 x 1'

Cerro Gordo
Miriam Sagan

The child says:
"A river, sometimes
it has water in it,
sometimes it doesn't..."

Not the rivers
I grew up with
But my daughter, born here,
Thinks of river
As dry course.

River did cut this canyon.
Wear down rock
Riddled with ancient shells
Mementos of a sea
Long ebbed away.

The poet Phil Whalen,
Zen priest,
Lived in the little temple here
By Cerro Gordo Park,
Stupa properly situated
Between a turtle-shaped hill
And a river. He used to say:
"One day
we'll just turn on the faucet
and sand will pour out..."

And once, when the kids were little,
My friend Hope and I
Scrambled down the bank
Took them hobo-ing
Along the weedy track
Until we tripped an electronic eye
Heard the canned voice warn:
GET BACK, GET BACK,
THE POLICE WILL BE CALLED.
We hadn't realized this way
Was anyone's private property.

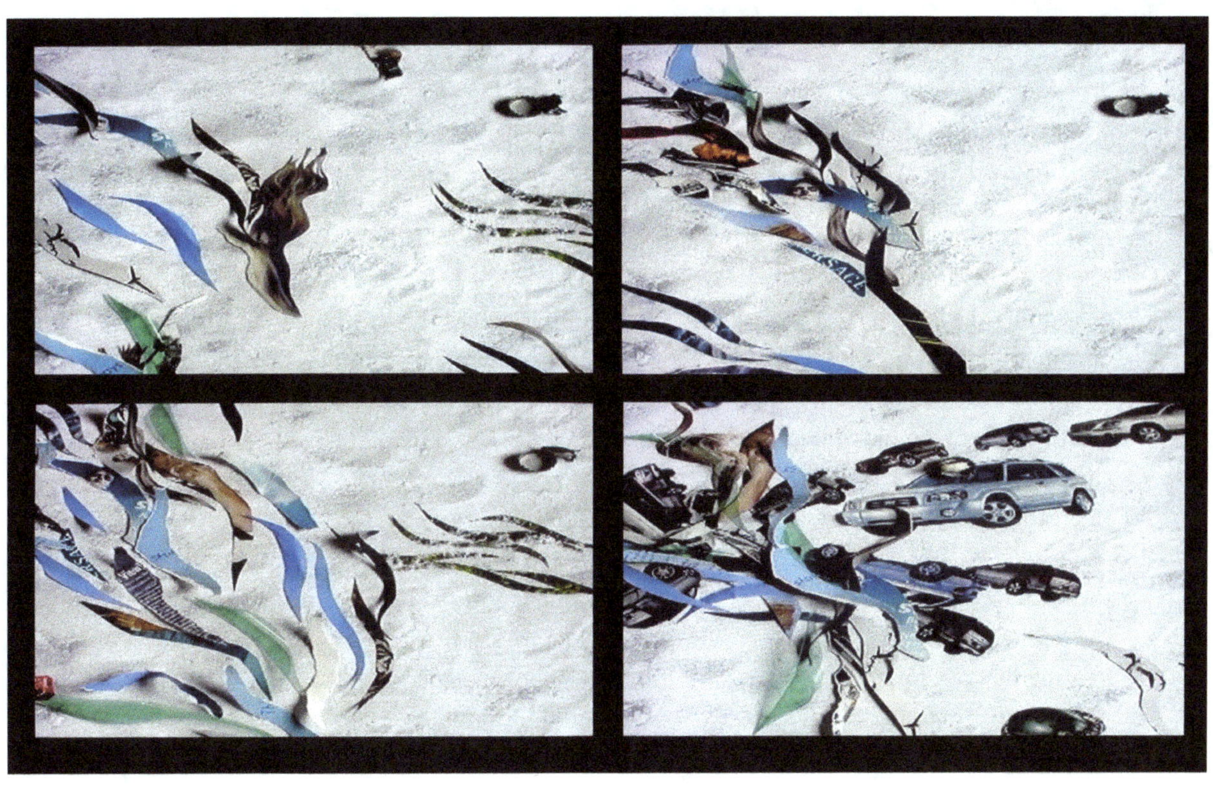

Edie Tsong, “Current,” animation video, variable dimensions

Sunday morning, early
Lorraine Schechter

the last sliver of moon says listen—
in this moment life is born;
the neighbors still dream
of winning the lottery
or something darker.
The cat returns with a mouse
squirming between his white incisors
cutting into flesh. I could hear
the tearing if I listened,

the cherry tree so fat with fruit
the branches drip
inviting first one bird
then another to taste.
The second cat, grey stripes flashing,
flies up the tree licking lips
I'd just noticed were delicate pink.

Under the grapevines
a bright orange globe
peeks over the horizon
and what was colorless is now
a thousand shades of green
the veined wonder called grape leaf
holding the light
rolling it across her vast
exquisitely shaped expanse
hiding plump clusters.

Hummingbirds hover at their red nectars—
scarlet runner beans, trumpet vines
a feeder with red dye
like a hooker in her red dress.

I listen for words to color
the extreme whiteness of the page
washed in the sounds of a fresh morning
a dog barks, a car revs its engine,
neighbors make love
and the emptiness
that isn't blank
is filled.

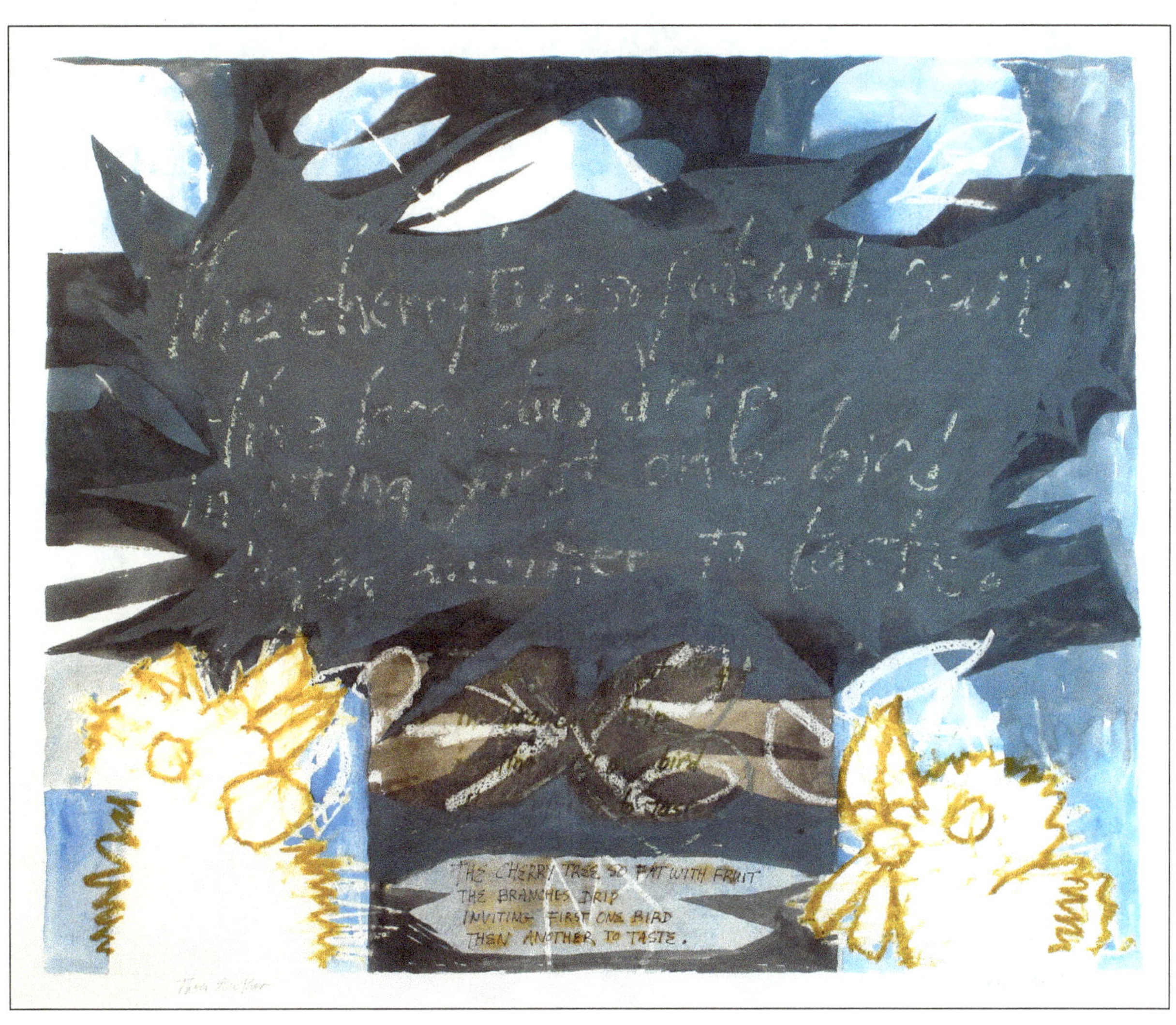

Peter Chapin, "Then Another," oil pastel/wax/gouache and pen on Rives BFK, 30 x 34"

FOUR A.M.
Henry Shukman

This is the hour the troubled man
hears the call of a train looping up a valley
and knows he must leave his home,
and also that he won't;

the hour the desperate wife
clutches her robe at the neck
and bathes herself in the light of a fridge,
having nowhere else to turn.

The poet looking out her window
at this hour see she must
resolve her loves once and for all,
but only writes another poem.

Already a big dog lifts its *woof* into the air.
Something smaller answers: *yap yap*.
Soon the stars will withdraw one by one,
and milk lighten the coffee, and there won't

be anything left but ordinary day.
No one would guess not an hour ago
creation lay open like the back of a watch
and an early waker saw it all.

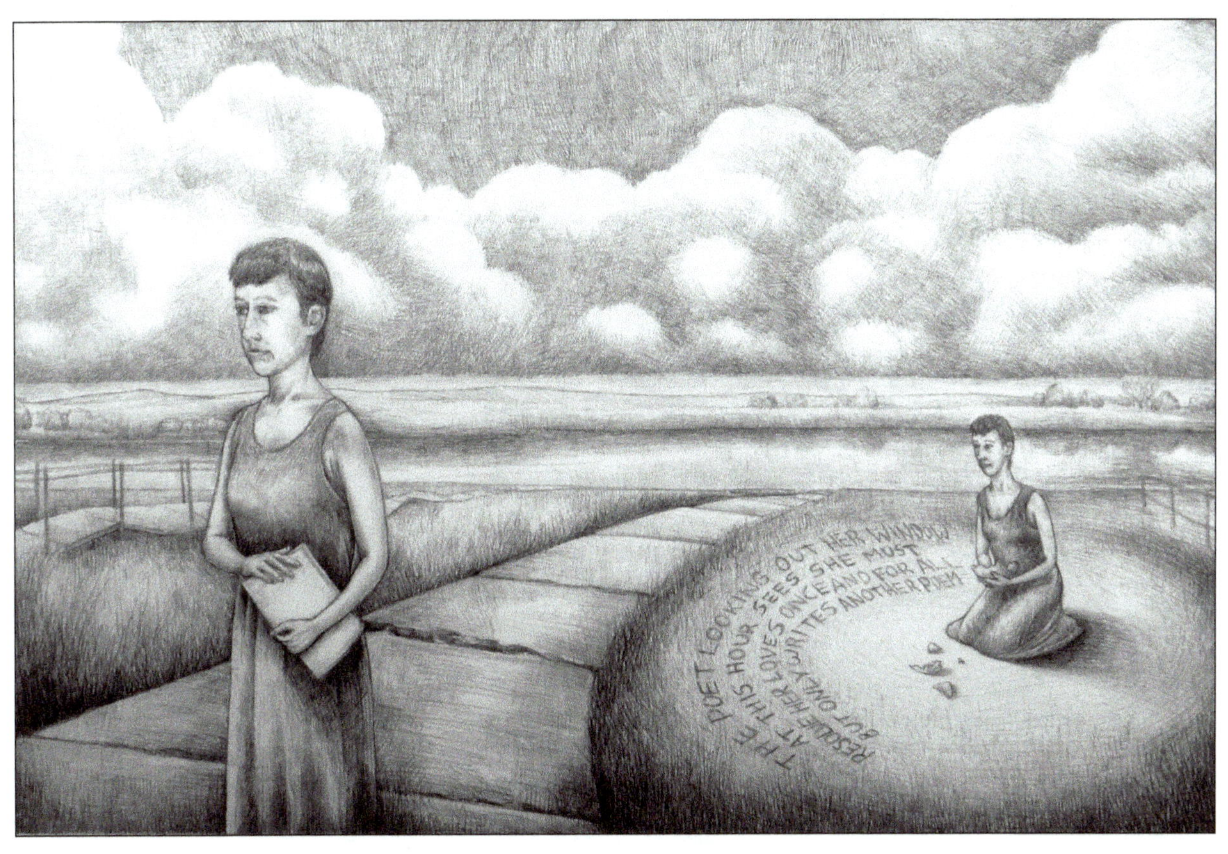

Andrew Keim, "The Poet," pencil on paper, 31 x 40"

haiku
Charles Trumbull

the aspens
and the chamisa agree
on a shade of yellow

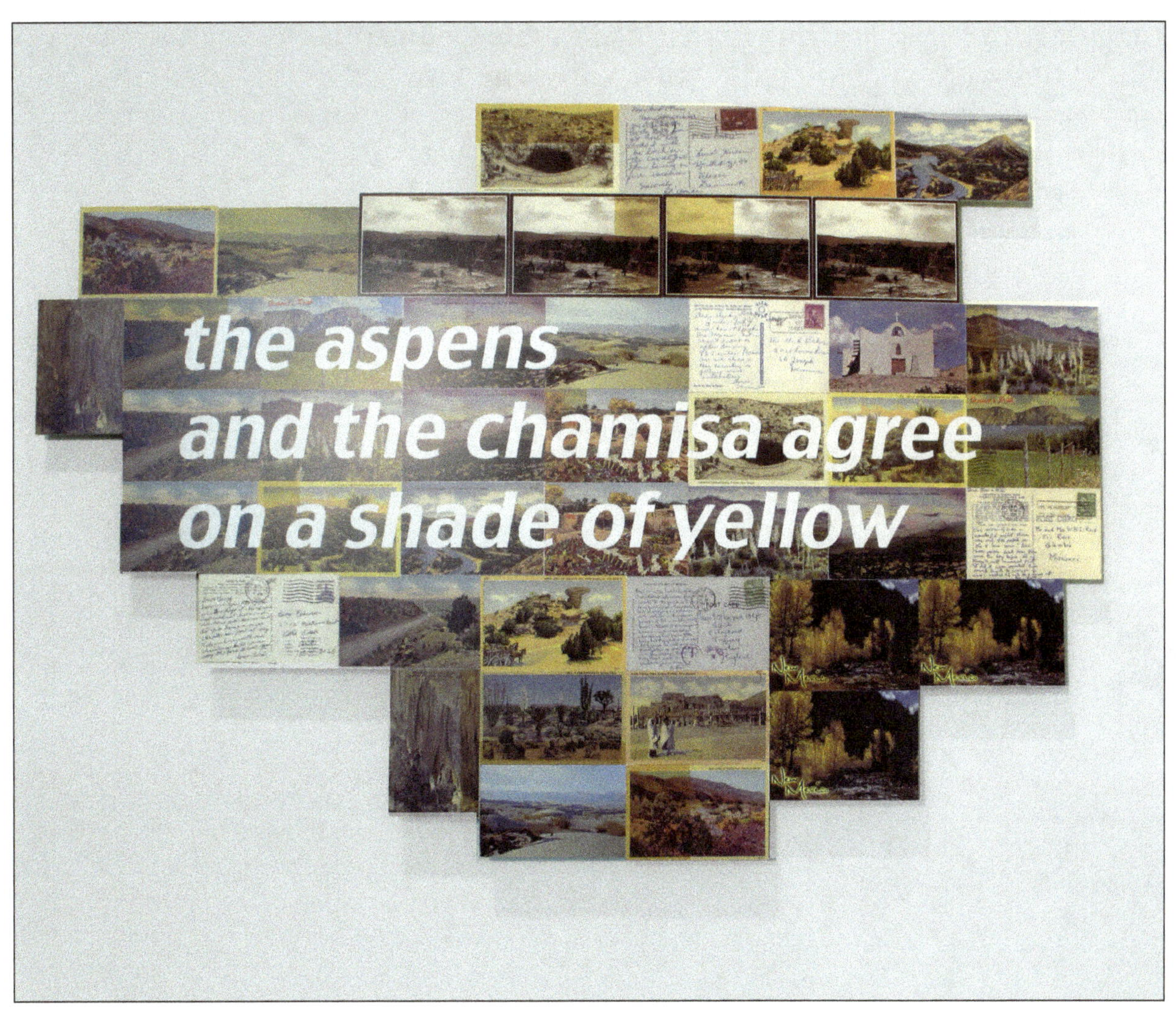

Donna Ruff, "Wish You Were Here," digital print mounted on cintra, 28 x 42"

Things That Want to Be Counted
Anne Valley-Fox

Someone on earth is counting—
night stars,
rooms in a honeycomb,
snow geese descending, wild
lilies, grain spilled from a bushel basket,
bubbles rising up from a blue hole.

Those who are hungry get up in the dark.
Their job is to count
sticks of kindling, cups of milk,
empty beds or racks of shoes,
newspapers in the dwindling stack,
how many fish in the bottom of the boat.

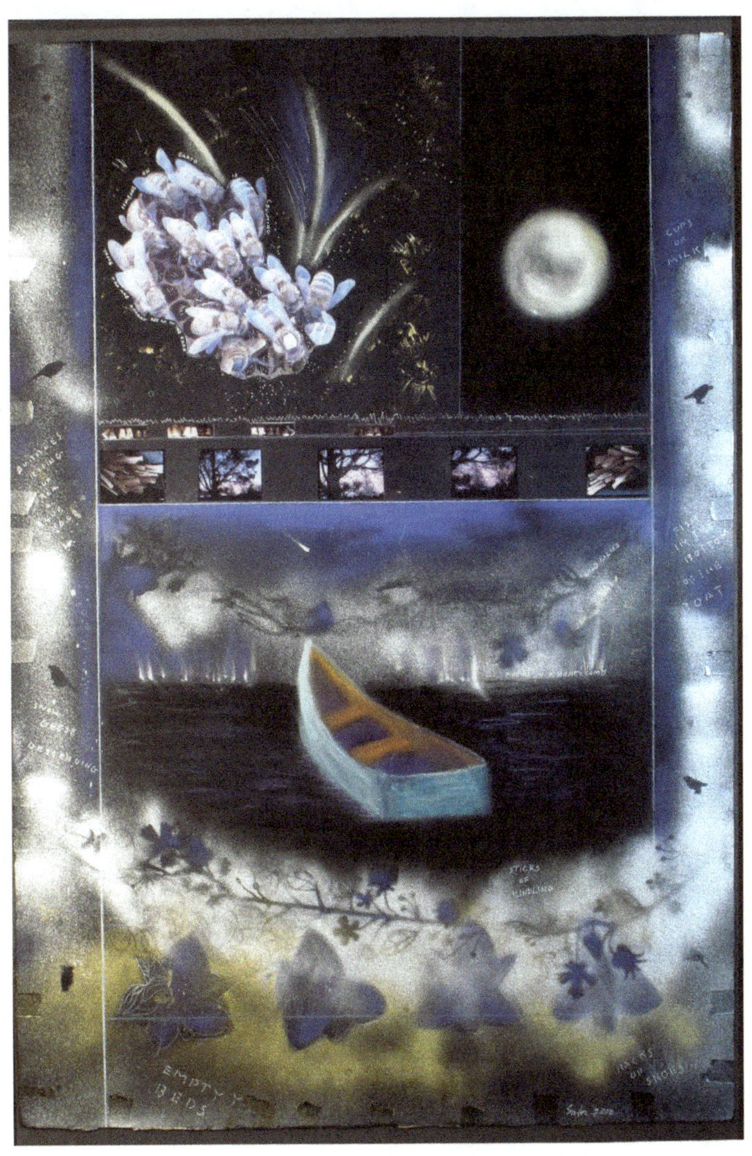

Nancy Sutor, "What Counts, 2012," photography/pastel/paint and tape on paper, 30 x 45"

Although I Live in Town Now
Cynthia West

Today the geese fly south
    bearing summer away on their wings.
    I stretch my hands to catch the cries

they let fall. Although I live in town now,
    with no tree to hold their sounds, I hear them
    in my sleep. The smell of dust raised by thunder
    lies stored in my dreams
    as well as fields of ripe corn.

Sticks tied with four colors touch the moon.
    Although I live in town now,
    my dance-ground waits where I hide it,

under the blue dome of August painted
    with the sunflowers of my people.
    Although the Santa Fe River

has dried up, I save a basket of clouds
    to sing into rain. I keep the ancient bowls
    to harvest the peaches. When I visit my shelves
    in winter, I will have plenty to eat.

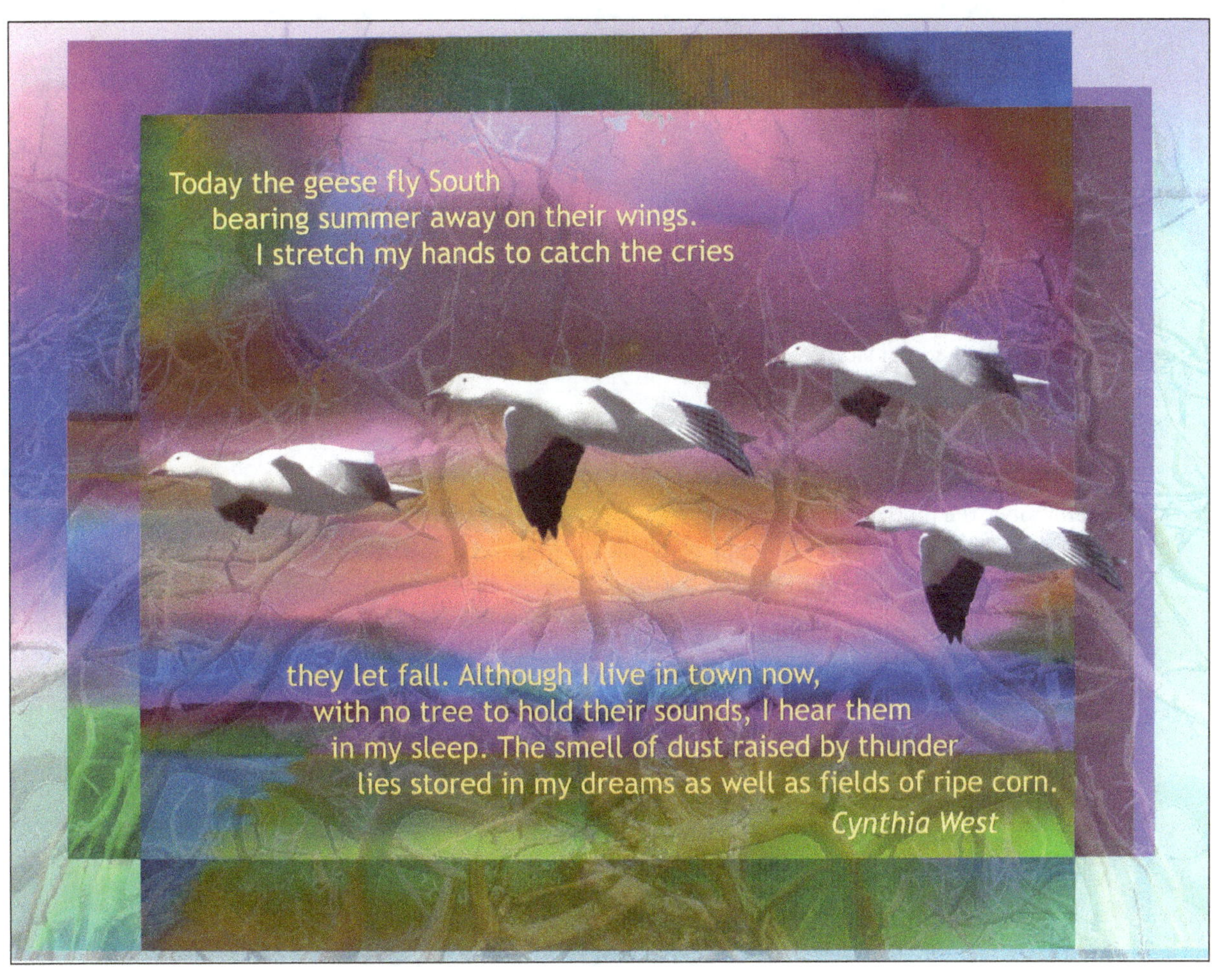

Ursula Freer, "Today the Geese Fly South," digital print, 16 x 21"

Thunder Clouds
Santana Shorty

I remember darkness.
A muffled handprint against my face.
The stale taste of cotton pressed to my lips, a bruising kiss goodnight.
It tasted like dried dreams and insomnia.
Like the underside of sleep.

Your hands molded my body into something I would eventually hate.
Appreciate nothing, flinching every time I saw my naked lines.
I remember the pillow.
A white bedtime story that turned black when I read it too close.
You drilled yourself into me.
The screws didn't fit but you forced them and I let you,
So screw me for being so naive and screw my screams,
My voice so loud, I couldn't hear myself anymore, couldn't see myself anymore,
So I cried, because maybe the salt water would puddle where I was lying and I could find my body again.
I cried, not because of what you did, but what I felt after.
I deserved this.
Deserved to be quieted by duct tape kisses, black and blue sweet dreams, unsober eyes painting pretty pictures, take a look at THIS piece of art.
Pieces of me scattered around the room.
You took every one of my limbs and licked it clean to the bone.
And here I thought monsters lived under the bed.

You broke me that night and I didn't realize it until the morning.
I saw my body lying in fragments around the room, decorated by condom wrappers.
I became an unwrapped present that was an old toy by now.
Wrappers and receipts.
There weren't any return policies on them.
I signed my heart away to you.
Signatured the sale of my self—respect and removed the For Sale sign from my ribcage.
I broke myself that night and didn't realize it until the morning.

I came across pages I had written to you.
Frozen moments, solid ice on paper.
Those feelings have thawed, mixed with my blood and tears and evaporated.
I hope they rain on you.
Give you goose bumps when it thunders during a storm.
And when it does, know that the water you feel on your face is me.
Know that you will never experience a drought because my eyes will bring the rain, my breath will create the wind and those hailstones you feel are these words I never said.
I'm saying them now.

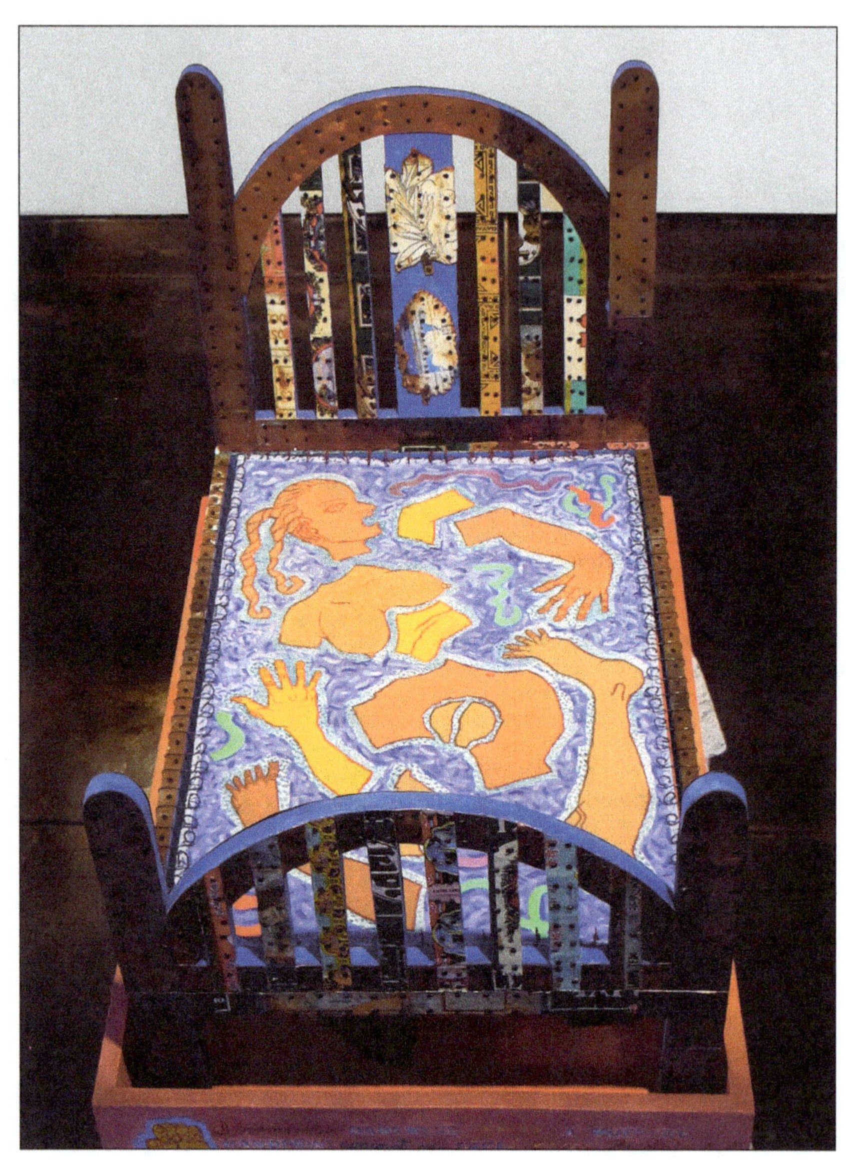

Sabra Moore, "Bedtime Story," oil on gessoed wood and paper/metal on wood/wire, 33 x 24 x 36"

Poet Biographies

(Websites and email addresses current as of the publication of the book.)

Tommy Archuleta is a native Santa Fean. He lives with his family in Cochiti Lake, New Mexico. With Dana Levin and Carol Moldaw he organizes the Muse Times Two Poetry Series at Collected Works Bookstore.

John Brandi has been faithful to the craft of poetry, painting and journaling for most of his life. He gave the keynote address for the Haiku North America conference in Ottawa Canada (2009), lectured on Matsuo Basho for Punjabi University, India (2010), and presented talks to celebrate his exhibit of poem-paintings at the Chavez History Museum, in Santa Fe (2011). He lives in El Rito, New Mexico, with his wife, poet Renée Gregorio. "After Li Ch'ing-chao" was published in *In What Disappears* (White Pine, 2003).

Debbi Brody conducts poetry workshops and readings at festivals and other venues throughout the Southwest to writers age twelve through eighty-five. She publishes frequently in regional and national literary journals. Her work has recently appeared in the *Santa Fe Literary Review, Broomweed Journal, Poetica, Sin Fronteras* and many others magazines and books of note including numerous anthologies. Debbi has lived in Santa Fe with her family since 1992. "Get Stirred" was previously published in *Book Lung; Poetry's Spin on Art* 09/2008.

Witter Bynner (1881–1968) Paul Horgan said, "A man of commanding stature, splendid good looks, and infectious energy, he presided over the cultural and convivial life in Santa Fe for five decades." Bynner graduated summa cum laude from Harvard, met such notables as D.H. and Frieda Lawrence, Mark Twain and Henry James. He proposed to Edna St. Vincent Millay and she accepted, but then they changed their minds. Steven Schwartz of the Witter Bynner Foundation for Poetry says, "He was a man. He was a poet. He was a translator. He was a playwright, an essayist, and a great correspondent." Bynner is the only non-living poet to be included in "Odes & Offerings" because through the Witter Bynner Foundation for Poetry his influence lives on in the great poetry climate his foundation has supported and has received a Santa Fe Mayor's Award for Art Excellence. "Santa Fe" was previously published in *Harold Witter Bynner, Uncollected Poems.*

Lauren Camp produces and hosts "Audio Saucepan," a music and poetry program that airs weekly on Santa Fe Public Radio. Her poems have recently appeared or are forthcoming in *Beloit Poetry Journal, Hotel Amerika, World Literature Today, Rhino* and other journals. The author of the poetry collection, *This Business of Wisdom* (West End Press) and a part-time educator, Lauren writes about poetry on her blog *Which Silk Shirt*. www.laurencamp.com/whichsilkshirt.

Sudasi J. Clement is the poetry editor for the *Santa Fe Literary Review*. Her poems have recently appeared in *Slipstream, Appalachee Review, Sierra Nevada Review*, and *The Mas Tequila Review.* Samples of Sudasi's poems and beadwork can be seen at beadpoet.com. "Eva and the Birds" first appeared in *Miriam's Well*, at www.miriamswell.wordpress.com.

Catherine Ferguson is a poet and painter. She creates watercolors, oils, *retablos,* and poems that express her love for nature. Catherine is the author of eight chapbooks. In 2007 she received the New Mexico Book Award in poetry for *The Sound a Raven Makes*, a collection with two other poets, Sawnie Morris and Michelle Holland. She is featured poet in Malpais Review, Autumn 2011 and won another New Mexico Book Award in 2011 in the religious category for her collaboration with Lisa Sandlin, *You Who Make the Sky Bend: Saints as Archetypes of the Human Condition*, Pinyon Publishing.

Phil Geronimo says, "A series of life changing experiences awoke the muses in me at the age of thirty-seven. With the assistance of my poetry mentor, Dan George, I was exposed to the best the poetry world has to offer. My three and one-half year stint at Collected Works Bookstore brought me into the poetry scene of Santa Fe at a level I could never have imagined."

Jenice Gharib's writing has appeared in publications such as *Vision Magazine*, *Not Enough Night*, and *Sin Fronteras.* Three of her plays, *Consorting with Angels, Some Kiss We Want* and *The Dressing Room*, have been produced. With Theaterwork, she appeared in and/or produced new work for *As Kingfishers Catch Fire: A Celebration of Poetry by Gerard Manley Hopkins*; *Such Stuff as Dreams are Made On*, a poetic response to Shakespeare's *The Tempest*; and *Other Antigones*, poetry inspired by Jean Anouilh's *Antigone*. She lives in Santa Fe.

Natalie Goldberg is the author of eleven books including *Writing Down the Bones*, which has been translated into fourteen languages. She teaches retreats on writing and Zen practice nationally but her main place is the Mabel Dodge Luhan house in Taos. She is also the author of a book entitled *True Secret*. "Dance With Me" was first published in *Chicken and in Love*, Holy Cow Press, 1980.

Renée Gregorio is the author of several published collections of poems, most recently *Drenched,* Fish Drum, Incorporated. She collaborates with Joan Logghe and Miriam Sagan as founders of Tres Chicas Books, their most recent title being a selection of poems from each: *Love & Death: Greatest Hits,* winner of a New Mexico Book Award in 2011. As a dedicated practitioner of aikido and a lover of language, Renée works as a master somatic coach, combining principles of aikido, poetry and somatics in individual and group work to help others achieve depthful expression and authorship of their work and lives. "Sometimes" first published in *Drenched,* Fish Drum, Incorporated, 2010.

Judyth Hill is a New Mexico poet, teacher, author, living wildly as ever, on her agave and bougainvillea bedecked ranchito, Simple Choice Farm, just outside San Miguel de Allende, Mexico. She has authored six poetry collections, a cookbook, innumerable magazine articles, the internationally acclaimed poem, "Wage Peace" and now leads WildWriting Culinary adventures around the world. www.eat-write-travel.com

Michelle Holland lives, runs, gardens, and writes in Chimayo, New Mexico with her husband Tom, a New Mexico landscape painter. Her most recent publications are *Chaos Theory*, Sin Fronteras Press, and *Event Horizon*, included in the New Mexico Book Award winning collection, *The Sound a Raven Makes*, Tres Chicas Press. "Daughters in Winter" was previously published in *Chaos Theory*, Sin Fronteras Press.

Kathamann is a retired R.N. and Peace Corps Volunteer in Afghanistan. She has been published in *Waving; Not Drowning, Sage Trail, The Rag, Lunarosity, Beatlick News, When Red Becomes an Apple, The House Where Numbers Slept, Small Canyons* II, III, IV, and V Anthology, *Chest,* Official publication of the American College of Chest Physicians, *Echoes, Malpais, The Enigmatist, Adobe Walls* II and III, and *Generations.*

Piper Leigh is a writer, photographer and bookmaker as well as a learning designer and educator. She sees poetry as a conversation, listening and giving voice to what is meaningful in the weave of story, community, and land. Whether through her work as a poet or as founding principal of Comunica Learning Partners, Piper is committed to inspiring courageous creativity to build a culture of connection in our world. Her recent book, *my thin-skinned wandering,* was published by Tres Chicas Books.

Past NEA Fellow **Donald Levering's** ninth and tenth books of poetry are *The Number of Names* and *Sweeping the Skylight.* He previously directed the Theaterwork Poetry Reading Series. He has been an Academy of American Poets Featured Poet in the Online Forum, was interviewed for the inaugural issue of *New Mexico Poetry Review,* and was profiled in the Ad Astra Poetry Project blog. "The Geese at Bosque Del Apache" was previously published in *Sin Fronteras/Writers Without Borders.* www.donaldlevering.com

Dana Levin is the author of three books, most recently *Sky Burial* (Copper Canyon Press). She co-chairs the Creative Writing and Literature Department at Santa Fe University of Art and Design. Excerpt from the poem "Pure Land" from *Sky Burial,* copyright 2011 by Dana Levin, used by permission of Copper Canyon Press. www.coppercanyonpress.org

Jane Lipman's chapbooks, both published by Pudding House Publications, were finalists for New Mexico Book Awards, *The Rapture of Tulips* in 2009 and *White Crow's Secret Life* in 2010. Her first full-length poetry collection, *On the Back Porch of the Moon*, was just published by Black Swan Editions, 2012.

Joan Logghe was Santa Fe's Poet Laureate 2010–2012. "Odes & Offerings" is her final project in this position. *The Singing Bowl* (University of New Mexico Press) and *Love & Death: Greatest Hits* (Tres Chicas Books) are her two recent books; the latter with Miriam Sagan and Renée Gregorio won a 2011 New Mexico Book Award for poetry. Joan has won a National Endowment for the Arts grant, years of support from the Witter Bynner Foundation for Poetry, and a Mabel Dodge Luhan Internship. www.joanlogghe.com thepoemdifferent.blogspot.com

Mary McGinnis has been writing, living, laughing and enjoying New Mexico since 1972. *Listening For Cactus* was published in 1996, and *October Again* was published in 2008. She was the first recipient of a *Poetry Gratitude Award* in 2009 from New Mexico Literary Arts. "Wild Pears" was previously published in *Listening for Cactus,* Sherman Asher Publishing, Santa Fe, New Mexico, 1996.

James McGrath, a Santa Fe Living Treasure, is a Santa Fe Sunstone Press published poet with three books of poetry; artist-poet in residence with United States Information Agency Arts America in Yemen, Republic of the Congo and Saudi Arabia. He hosts poetry readings in his apple orchard. In 2012 he won a Poetry Gratitude Award from New Mexico Literary Arts. His biography, *James McGrath: In a Class by Himself* by Jonah Raskin, published by McCaa Books is out now.

Carol Moldaw is the author of five books of poems, most recently *So Late, So Soon: New and Selected Poems* (Etruscan Press, 2010) and *The Widening,* a novel. In the spring of 2011 she served as the Louis D. Rubin, Jr., Writer-in-Residence at Hollins University. "Our New Life" is a selection from *Chalkmarks on Stone.*

Mary Morris is the winner of the Rita Dove Award and the New Mexico Discovery Award. She has been a guest poet at the Library of Congress and publishes widely. "Acupuncture with Dr. Hao" was first published in *Poet Lore.*

Elizabeth Raby is the author of three full-length poetry collections, *The Year the Pears Bloomed Twice,* 2009, *Ink on Snow,* 2010, and *This Woman,* 2012, all published by Virtual Artists Collective (www.vacpoetry.org) and of three chapbooks. Her poem, "Bride-to-Be" won the 2010 Kelton Contest, sponsored by Angelo State University, San Angelo, Texas. She worked as a poet-in-the-schools in Pennsylvania and New Jersey and for the Geraldine R. Dodge Foundation before moving to Santa Fe in 2000. "At the Wheel of the Year" appeared in the 2010 Texas Poetry Calendar, and in *Ink on Snow,* published by Virtual Artists Collective, 2010.

Stella Reed has been living, writing, singing and loving in Santa Fe, New Mexico for over twenty-three years. She has won awards locally and nationally for her poetry and fiction and has been published in anthologies and journals in the United States and Australia.

Barbara Robidoux's poetry is widely published nationwide in anthologies and journals. She also has published a full-length poetry collection, *Waiting for Rain.* She has written a collection of short stories about life on a northeastern Indian reservation where she lived before relocating to Santa Fe eighteen years ago. Another collection of haiku, tanka and haibun, *Migrant Moon*, was launched in April, 2012.

Barbara Rockman teaches poetry at Santa Fe Community College and in private workshops. Her prize-winning poems appear widely in literary journals and anthologies. She is author of the chapbook, *Surrender To Storm*, and the collection of poetry, *Sting and Nest (Sunstone Press).* She is editor of the anthology, *Women Becoming Poems.* Barbara earned her Masters of Fine Art in Writing from Vermont College of Fine Arts. "Letter from Georgia O'Keeffe To Alfred Stieglitz Upon Seeing His Photograph Of Her Hands" first appeared in *Louisville Review.*

Leo Romero has been a bookseller in Santa Fe since 1988. Current bookstore: Books of Interest. Previous bookstores: Books and More Books, Leo's Art Books & Music, and Leo's Books. Leo has completed a fiction manuscript, *Crazy for Fabiola*. "Una Canción de Flores" appeared in *The Indian Rio Grande: Recent Poems From 3 Cultures,* San Marcos Press.

Levi Romero, is the Centennial Poet of New Mexico and author of *A Poetry of Remembrance: New and Rejected Works*, and *In the Gathering of Silence*. His collaborative photodocumentary book, *SAGRADO: A Photopoetics Across the Chicano Homeland*, is published by the University of New Mexico Press. "Juxtaposition" is a selection from *A Poetry of Remembrance: New and Rejected Works*, University of New Mexico Press.

Miriam Sagan founded and directs the creative writing program at the Santa Fe Community College, including the student run *Santa Fe Literary Review* and the permanent poetry showcase installation Poetry Posts. In 2010, she received the Santa Fe Mayor's Award for Excellence in the Arts. She is currently working extensively with Center for Land Use Interpretation in Wendover, Utah. Some of her writing was the basis of a gallery show at 516 Arts in Albuquerque, 2012.

Lorraine Schechter received her Masters of Fine Arts in graphics and painting from the University of Pennsylvania School of Design, where she was later given an Angell Post-Graduate fellowship in Graphics. She lived in the south of France and the hills of northwestern Connecticut where she was manager of the Alexander Calder home and studio before settling in Santa Fe in 1988. *The Seasons of Yes: Poems and Images* from Sunstone Press won the 2008 New Mexico Book Award in Poetry. A teacher and arts administrator for forty years, Lorraine recently completed her public contracts to return full time to the studio where she has worked on a series of mixed media paintings and prints called *One Earth.* Her work can be seen online at www.lorraineschechter.com. "Sunday morning, early" is from *Seasons of Yes: Poems and Images.*

Santana Shorty is a young Navajo artist from Abiquiu, New Mexico. She is most well-known for her work with the Santa Fe Indian School Spoken Word Team, an organization she was a part of for six years. Through Spoken Word, Santana traveled nationally and internationally, sharing her personal and cultural stories in the form of performance poetry. In 2009 she was the New Mexico *Poetry Out Loud* State Champion, traveling to the National Finals in Washington, DC.

Henry Shukman's first poetry collection, *In Dr No's Garden* (Cape, 2002), was Book of the Year in the *Guardian* and *Times* (London). He was Poet in Residence at the Wordsworth Trust, and Royal Literary Fund Poetry Fellow at Oxford Brookes University, and now lives in New Mexico, where he writes for *The New York Times* and sometimes teaches at the Institute of American Indian Arts. His novels include *The Lost City* (Knopf, 2008), which was *Guardian* Book of the Year and a *New York Times* Editor's Choice. His second poetry collection, *Archangel,* is forthcoming in early 2013 from Cape/Random House. "Four A.M." was previously published in *Granta – British Council, New Writing 15.*

Charles Trumbull left home in northern New Mexico for almost fifty years to pursue a career in international communications, notably writing, editing, and publishing, latterly at Encyclopædia Britannica. Now back, he edits the journal *Modern Haiku* in Santa Fe.

Major geographical hubs for **Anne Valley-Fox** include Paterson, New Jersey, Santa Monica, California, Berkeley, California, and, for the past thirty-five years, the enchanted lands of northern New Mexico. Her poetry books include *How Shadows Are Bundled* (University of New Mexico

Press, 2009), *Point of No Return* (La Alameda Press, 2004), *Fish Drum 15* (Fish Drum Press, 1999) and *Sending the Body Out* (Zephyr Press, 1986). Please see AnneValleyFox.com. "Things That Want to Be Counted" is from *How Shadows Are Bundled*, University of New Mexico Press. She is also the compiler and editor, along with Ann Lacy, of a series of books based on material from the New Mexico Federal Writers' Project from Sunstone Press.

Known for her visionary paintings, **Cynthia West** is also a poet, photographer, digital imager and book artist. Her Santa Fe home with many gardens, where she has lived for forty years with her husband and family, is a healing center as well as her studio and gallery. Her works are collected world-wide. She is the author of five previous collections of poetry, *For Beauty Way, 1000 Stone Buddhas, Rainbringer, The New Sun,* and *In the Center of the Field*, the last three from Sunstone Press. Visit her website at www.westvision.us. "Although I Live in Town Now" was first published in *In the Center of the Field,* Sunstone Press, 2010.

Artist Biographies

(Websites and email addresses current as of the publication of the book.)

Bobbe Besold's primary focus is to create art for Earth's sake, in part by engaging, educating, and collaborating with others in all media. Her art and design work (called Watershed) was cast into concrete walls for a pedestrian underpass for the City of Santa Fe. www.bobbebesold.com.

Joy Campbell is a native New Mexican who chose Santa Fe as her retirement community. Following a teaching career, Joy found her passion for making books, both bound constructions as well as altered books. Her book art can be seen at ViVO Contemporary Gallery on Canyon Road and The City of Santa Fe Arts Commission Community Gallery on Marcy Street in Santa Fe, New Mexico. www.joymcampbellbookartist.com

Dawn Chandler was born and raised in New Jersey, but found her heart and soul in New Mexico. She studied painting at Miami University of Ohio, earned her Master of Fine Art at the University of Pennsylvania, and attended the Skowhegan School of Painting and Sculpture in Maine. Dawn lived in Taos for fifteen years before moving to Santa Fe in 2009.

Peter Chapin studied with John Heliker, Philip Guston and others at Columbia for his Master of Fine Arts degree. He chaired the Art Department at Drew University and helped found the Printmaking Center of New Jersey. Living in Santa Fe for the past twenty-five years he has continued to paint, teach and volunteer with various organizations.

Born in 1965, in Cambridge, Massachusetts, **Matthew Chase-Daniel** earned a Bachelor of Art from Sarah Lawrence College in 1987. His explorations in art have taken him from his grandmother's knee (abstract expressionism) to the coasts of the Pacific Northwest (native carving), and Paris, France (filmmaking at the Ecole Pratique des Hautes Etudes). He has lived with his wife Julie, in Santa Fe, New Mexico since 1989, making things ranging from photography to sculpture, drawings, fireplaces, and a son. Chase-Daniel is the co-founder of Axle Contemporary, which facilitates alternative art exhibitions in a mobile gallery based in Santa Fe.

Chicago-born **Bernadette Freeman** is a recent arrival in Santa Fe, New Mexico, bringing with her collage and assemblage compositions unexplored by other paper artists. Specializing in tiny images and words cut from magazines and mail order catalogs, Freeman's self-developed technique swirls color, word, shape and humor. Her pieces included her own poetry as well as the words of James Joyce, Abraham Lincoln, Stevie Smith, and Joan Logghe.

Trained as a painter in the classical tradition **Ursula Freer** started working with the digital medium seventeen years ago. For her, the digital tools have opened up greater possibilities for creative expression. Working with images is her way to experience, gain insights and communicate these concepts about how things work on the levels of consciousness, nature and the universe.

Charles Greeley, an exhibiting artist in the Santa Fe art scene for the past forty years creates visionary landscape collages out of Japanese printed papers as well as "Transcendental" abstract paintings. His art is in the permanent collections of major contemporary art museums including The New Mexico Museum of Art. He is currently represented by Mill Fine Art on Canyon Road, Santa Fe, New Mexico and had a one person show of new paintings in 2012.

Roger Green is a native Chicagoan. There he was a graphic designer, taught Visual Arts at the Illinois Institute of Art, and founded his own full-service advertising agency. Roger moved to Albuquerque, New Mexico in 2005 where he continues to paint and exhibit his art full time.

Andrew Keim has been drawing for many years and received his Bachelor of Fine Art at San Diego State University in 1995, and his Master of Fine Art at the New York School of Visual Arts in 1997. He moved to Albuquerque in 2002, and then to Santa Fe in 2005. www.andrewkeim.com

For over three decades, **Shirley Klinghoffer**, artist/activist, has exhibited her sculpture in museums and galleries worldwide. She was recently honored for her "feminist artwork" with a mini retrospective, curated by Laura Addison, New Mexico Museum of Art Contemporary Curator, at Judy Chicago's Through the Flower Foundation gallery. Klinghoffer's work is included in numerous public and private collections, and in 2010 she was nominated for the New Mexico Governor's Award for Excellence in the Arts with special tributes to her nationwide collaborative project "Love Armor Project." www.shirleyklinghoffer.com, www.lovearmorproject.com

Painter and printmaker **Ann Laser** discovered her passion for art after raising a family and spending twenty-plus years as a psychotherapist. A native Arkansan, she attended the University of Arkansas where she was first exposed to formal art classes. Currently she makes her home in Santa Fe, New Mexico. Ann uses her intuition in combining color, form and layering to create work that reflects a push—pull tension between the seen/unseen, surface/depth, and conscious/unconscious. www.annlasercontemporaryart.com

Piper Leigh is a writer, photographer and bookmaker as well as a learning designer and educator. She sees poetry as a conversation, listening and giving voice to what is meaningful in the weave of story, community, and land. She publishes artist books, participates in collaborative projects, and creates installations using different forms: cloth, scrolls, kimonos, mobiles. Whether through her work as an artist or Comunica, Piper is committed to inspiring courageous creativity to build a culture of connection in our world. www.piperleigh.us poetry and art www.comunica.com learning designer piperleigh@comunica.com

Thelma Mathias' embroidery work or drawing with thread, is a peculiar body of work to emerge as a dominant one in the past few years, out of more than thirty years as mainly a conceptual sculptor. Having lived in Santa Fe for the past ten years, Thelma's work is a natural outgrowth of many years of travel, exhibits and residencies in Mexico, while New York City was the birth place and home/studio.

Kathleen McCloud lives and works in rural La Cienguilla, "the little marsh," southwest of Santa Fe, New Mexico. "Predictable, slow-moving seasonal cycles, overseen by petroglyphs carved into volcanic rocks that are over a million years old, counter-balance the high frequency of digital communication that is as prevalent in my life as the blue sky. For grounding I look to the earth—the animated landscape has its own story and keeps informing my work. Making things is the way I listen, behold the paradox, and continue the story." www.kathleenmccloud.com

Sabra Moore is a Texas-born artist living in Abiquiu, New Mexico. Her work is based on re-interpreting family, social and natural history through the form of artist's books, sewn and painted "constructed" sculptures and wall works, and installations. She has exhibited extensively in New York City, Canada, Brazil and New Mexico and is committed to the idea of placing artwork within a social context. Her work is a kind of personal archaeology; she sees herself as a "literate" granddaughter who has synthesized the quiltmaking/storytelling traditions of her rural grandmothers into new forms.

Kuzana Ogg was born in Bombay. Her work in oil is influenced by the colors and patterns of her childhood, combined with those encountered on subsequent travels. She has exhibited work both nationally and internationally; including at our embassies in Latvia and Belize.

Janet O'Neal is a nationally recognized painter, printmaker, sculptor and mixed media artist. Her works are part of numerous corporate and private collections throughout the United States including IBM, Duke Energy, and Price Waterhouse. She is known for her energetic, colorful abstracts and figurative assemblages.

Sallyann Milam Paschall is a versatile, award-winning artist who resides in Santa Fe, New Mexico. The colors of the high deserts and mountains inform her work, as well as the Cherokee syllabry and the elegance of line found in great historical drawings. Her work may be seen each year at the Santa Fe Indian Market, the Heard Indian Art Market and the Cherokee Art Market, as well as the Berlin Gallery at the Heard Museum in Phoenix and the Lloyd Kiva New Gallery at the Museum of Contemporary Native Arts in Santa Fe.

Gail Rieke is an internationally recognized collage/assemblage/installation artist and teacher who lives and works in Santa Fe, New Mexico. She shows her work at her home/studio/gallery by appointment as well as at museums, galleries, and art centers. She teaches workshops nationally and internationally related to creative response to travel. www.riekestudios.com

Brenda Roper spent over twenty years in Alaska before moving to the oldest artist colony on Canyon Road in Santa Fe. She indulges her creative life by crossing borders, painting large, writing small and taking photos to mark her path. Her work is published in *Calyx A Journal of Art &*

Literature by Women, and *Cirque.* To read her blog or view her art please visit www.contemporary-artinsantafe.com.

Donna Ruff uses the processes of cutting and burning paper to reveal and obscure text and pattern. She often works with existing printed pages such as newspaper and book spreads. For "Odes & Offerings," she collected vintage postcards. Her work has been exhibited in galleries and museums in the United States as well as in India, Germany, Spain, Australia and the Czech Republic.

Jane Shoenfeld moved to Santa Fe in 1987; she grew up in the Northeast and continues to exhibit her pastel and mixed media nature abstractions through the First Street Gallery in New York City. Recently her abstract Gridscapes were featured on the covers of *The New Mexico Poetry Review* and *The Number of Names,* a collection of poetry by Donald Levering. Her work has been included in exhibitions through the Smithsonian Institute, Las Cruces Museum, Millicent Rogers Museum, Brooklyn Museum and is also collected in New Mexico through purchase awards through New Mexico Art in Public Places.

Carol Sky earned a University of Houston Bachelor of Fine Art, University of Iowa Master of Art and Master of Fine Art, studied at the Corcoran College of Art, and the Slade school of Art in London, England. While teaching and working in universities and museums and galleries, she has had more than twenty-four solo and over two hundred juried shows in the United States, China, Austria, Cuba and San Salvador. She has work in The National Museum of Women in the Arts, and in private, public and corporate collections in the United States, England, India and Brazil.

Michael Stone is a photographer and a digital artist with a Master of Fine Arts Degree from the University of California at Los Angeles (1971). His art has appeared in the Museum of Modern Art, New York, the Albuquerque Museum of Art, Albuquerque, New Mexico, and was represented in Pacific Standard Time at Cherry and Martin Gallery in Los Angeles, California in 2011. His art is in the permanent collections of the Washington State Arts Commission, the Norton Simon Art Museum, Pasadena, California and the National Gallery of Art in Washington, DC.

Nancy Sutor has lived in New Mexico since the late 1970s, working in photography and drawing. She is interested in the cycle of the seasons and how things aren't always what they seem.

Bunny Tobias is a multi-media artist who has been exhibiting her art in major Santa Fe galleries for the past forty years. Her work includes ceramic sculpture, paintings, found object art and mixed-media jewelry. Her ceramic art is in the permanent collection of the New Mexico Museum of Art and her current interest is in expressing her conceptual ideas in the different mediums in which she works.

Edie Tsong is interested in how we relate to one another and how we relate to our environment. Her interdisciplinary explorations use video, performance, plasticene, teleconference, clay, and other everyday materials. She lives and works in Santa Fe. www.edietsong.com

Blair Vaughn-Gruler holds a Bachelor of Fine Art in painting from Northern Michigan University, and a Master of Fine Art in Visual Art from Vermont College of Fine Art. She lives and works in Lamy, New Mexico, and is co-owner of GVG Contemporary in Santa Fe. www.blair-vaughngruler.com, www.gvgcontemporary.com

Suzanne Vilmain lives in the Rio Grande valley with Black Mesa in view, making books, printing ephemera, connecting dominoes. Counting Coup Press / www.suzanne@vilmain.net

After **Julie Wagner** earned a Bachelor of Art from Oberlin College and a Master of Fine Art in Sculpture from the Rhode Island School of Design, she moved to northern New Mexico in 1972. Julie has been working in sculpture, drawing and making one-of-a-kind artists' books ever since. Her work is in public and private collections across the United States and Europe.

Cynthia West, known for painting, poetry, photography, digital imaging, and book arts, is the author five collections of poetry, *For Beauty Way*, 1990, and *1000 Stone Buddhas*, 1993, published by Inked Wingbeat, Santa Fe and *Rainbringer*, 2004, *The New Sun*, 2007 and *In the Center of the Field*, 2010, the last three published by Sunstone Press, Santa Fe. Visit her web-site: www.westvision.us.

Melanie West was born and raised in Santa Fe, New Mexico. Her work in both photography and filmmaking has been influenced by her large family, plenty of dancing and music, a respect and ability for work with one's hands, and the desert space around her. She was included in the

Through The Lens exhibit at The Palace of the Governors in Santa Fe and her work is in the prize-winning book. www.melaniewestphotography.com

Ruth Weston has been a clay sculptor for many years. She does figurative work which is feminist in its inspiration. She has moved away from aesthetic modernism which places great emphasis on form and instead includes content, feminine issues, in her art. www.ruthweston.com

S.K. Yeatts has degrees from Baylor University and the University of Texas. He formerly served as the Executive Director leading the User-Experience and Graphic Design group for AT&T. He moved to Santa Fe to focus full-time on literary publications of next-generation Poetry concepts and the production of limited edition 'Metalogical' photographic art.

Acknowledgements

The City of Santa Fe Arts Commission would like to thank: Sunstone Press for their interest and support of *Odes & Offerings* as a valuable exhibit and print-worthy book; Alex Traube for documenting the exhibit for presentation in these pages; Joan Logghe for her development and contributions to the success of this exhibit; Santa Fe University of Art and Design for their contribution to support Gallery programming during this exhibit; and The Witter Bynner Foundation for Poetry for their support of the Poet Laureate Program.

www.ingramcontent.com/pod-product-compliance
Lightning Source LLC
LaVergne TN
LVHW081252100826
845148LV00009B/1206

* 9 7 8 0 8 6 5 3 4 9 5 5 1 *